Your cell phone is ringing; it's a blocked number. You have no idea who it is, or what they want. But you know it's urgent, a matter of life or death, of maintaining the existence of the world as you know it today. This person knows you have bought this book. They know you are on a quest to become a SuperHero and they need you right this moment. There is no time to read, to learn, or to train. This is your call to adventure...

Answer the Call

How to Become a

⇩

Super

Hero

⇨ *BY* *SAGE MICHAEL*

SuperHero Press

Visit our website: www.SuperHeroPress.com

While the author has made every possible attempt to provide accurate tele-phone numbers and Internet addresses at the time of publication, neither the publisher nor the author assume any responsibility for errors or for changes that occur after publication. Further, the publisher does not have any control over and does not assume any responsibility for author or third-party websites or their content.

Publisher's Cataloging-in-Publication data available upon request.

ISBN 978-0-692-00109-7

Consult a physician before you begin this or any strenuous exercise pro-gram or diet modification, especially if you have, or suspect you may have, heart disease, high blood pressure, diabetes, or any other adverse medical conditions.

WARNING: If you feel faint or dizzy at any time while performing any por-tion of this training program, stop immediately and seek medical evaluation.

Printed in China.

Cover Art by Craig Bruyn

Book Design by Cecilia Sorochin/ SoroDesign
Typesetting Frutiger Light 9/12 combined with Clarendon

To
Celeste & Jordyn,
my first two Heroes.

Thank you for the inspiration.

But also to You,
my newest reader,
for the World you will create.

By my love and hope I beseech you:
Do not throw away the hero in your soul!
Hold holy your highest hope!

—Friedrich Nietzsche

Acknowledgments

How does one repay debts of gratitude at this order of magnitude? Surely I do not know. There are of course my daughters, who have provided me with all the motivation a person could ever want. When you look into the eyes of your children you mustn't come up lacking. I hope this work lives up to the magic of their dreams and meets with their approval.

Stan Lee, who absolutely deserves more than just a mention, but I fear that my words could never convey the worth I would like to express. Stan's characters have always been based on real people, and have continually hinted at our true potential (an idea I expound on further in the book). His work has not only inspired me, but has also guided me through the process. I don't know what Stan was thinking the first time I spoke to him on the phone, but I do know what I was thinking: How can a person this friendly, this *normal*, actually be the same person that keeps us so in awe? (Well, ok... I was also thinking: Oh My God, It's Stan Lee!!!)

My mom, who has had more to do with my being bold and brave than I realized until this writing. My dad who keeps thanking me for things even though I owe him way more than he could ever owe me. Seema who took care of so many side issues for me so that I could focus on the key things in my life that needed to get done (and who also put up with me for years) so that I could make it to this point.

Rosalind, for two years so inseparable that I was unsure even what to say about you in this section. For days then weeks then months you gave so much of yourself to this process that even a light read triggers the memories of our conversations. It was a long and beautiful road that we walked and, quite honestly, I haven't the tools to fathom all you've given me. It was amazing. Thank you.

George Hundleby and Melanie Vanderwood... though I am sure they do not know why. I will send a free copy of this book to the person who first helps me reestablish contact with them again. If you're interested: good luck. Here's a tip: they were in Southern California the last time I saw them.

My team of editors, stronger-willed than indomitable Poseidon, top-to-bottom scouring tumultuous seas, have extracted perhaps the only salvageable work therein. I hope, at long last, that they have wrung out at least a teaspoonful of life-giving water.

Craig Bruyn, a very gifted illustrator and Ceci Sorochin, a book designer without equal. It is their work that now emblazons the cover of this book, and that is likely the reason you have it in your hands today. Without them, where would we be? You both are amazing. Thank you.

Yaiza, You ask of me the impossible: Compress down everything I would think, feel, desire, remember, and love into naught but a single sentence. To say only what I must whilst avoiding the areas of conflagration. Sooner that you had set me to battle at least where I were forearmed. Yet indeed, if it must be this way, please accept my sentence thus: If only...

Table of Contents

PART II
SuperHero Boot Camp 127

10. The Only Easy Day Was Yesterday— 129

PART III
Super Powers 141

11. The Heart of it All— 143

It was just a matter of time!

Superhero thrillers top the list of Hollywood's blockbuster movies. Superhero costumes are among the biggest Halloween sellers. Superhero comic books command the highest prices at pop culture auctions and, to no one's surprise, the public can't seem to get enough of superhero toys, action figures and video games.

So what could be more natural than a book for anyone and everyone who's into the superhero mystique and nurses a secret desire to have the right stuff, superhero-wise? What could be more appealing to the countless legions of worldwide fans than a book that shows how to unleash the hidden superhero inside of you?

"How to Become a SuperHero" is undoubtedly the right book for the right time. As you read it, you may not be able to leap over a skyscraper with a single bound but, guided by Sage Michael's compelling and thought-provoking text, it may make you feel like a superhero by showing you how to do the best you can, how to be the best you can and how to serve as a role model for others, as every superhero should.

Now isn't that a goal worth striving for?

Excelsior!

STAN LEE

Preface

⇨

There is an incredible phenomenon sweeping the world at this very moment. It is the inevitable forward march of the SuperHero. Think about it: There are SuperHero movies, television shows and countless comic books. SuperHeroes are covered in mainstream magazines, the subject of novels, featured on websites and serve as pitchmen in advertisements. A worldwide movement has prompted a shift in how we view these crusaders. It seems the SuperHero is not only here to stay—they are here to take over.

This is an opportunity for you to jump in and be part of this exciting new direction. Don't just sit by and watch. Get up and get moving. To become a SuperHero means more than just buying into some fad or jumping on a bandwagon.

To become a SuperHero is to change your life; to take charge of it; to empower it. This is an opportunity not to be missed.

If you continue on this journey you will find yourself immersed in adventure. This is a guarantee. But it will only apply if you follow all of the exercises and commit to completing them to the best of your ability. If the book suggests you write something, write it. Don't just imagine it. There is power in seeing the words in front of you. And there is power in completion. This is your chance to change the world. This is no jest. This is a promise.

Why this book? Why now? These are easy questions. Victor Hugo once said that, "Nothing, not even the armies of the night, can stop an idea whose time has come." The real question here is not "Why this book?" The real question here then is "Why you?" Why does the world—your world—suddenly need you? What is it that you are being called to do?

I ask you not to read my work and judge for yourself. I am my own judge and I set my own direction. I ask instead that you be your own judge and jury, and when the time is right, that you execute your plans with the burning focus of laser sight.

Become more. Until now you have been the sleeping SuperHero. Awaken! You are being called to action.

(PART I)

⇩

SuperHero Theory

Your First Response

What if the call from the first page of the book really had come in? What would you have done? Why exactly were you called? What is it that lies within you? What great power is it you have yet to harness?

⇨

You knew the answer to these questions long before you ever picked up this book. That knowledge was inside you. There is clearly some reason that all of this is happening. Consider again the reason that you were being called in this urgent matter of life or death.

THIS PERSON CALLED YOU. THEY KNOW THAT YOU, THE SUPER-HERO, CAN HELP...BUT WITH WHAT? ANSWER IT NOW.

....

....

....

With this idea firmly in your mind, who is it that is calling you? Is it some special team? A secret organization? The government? A non-profit? In the deep corners of your mind, you already know.

WHO IS IT THAT NEEDS YOU FOR THIS MISSION?
WRITE IT DOWN:

....

Now begin to let this idea flourish inside your head. You can stop writing for now, but mentally fill in the missing details of this story. This is important. If you want to be a SuperHero, you will need to be creative. These first, initial thoughts are the single best representation of what kind of SuperHero you want to be and of the course you want this book to help you take. This instinctual response, your gut reaction, is the first step you will take in this journey of becoming a SuperHero. There will be many more before we are finished, but you will always want to be able to recall this initial imagery at any time. As was already mentioned, this step will help you choose.

What to Expect

A First Look at a SuperHero Book

This book will show you powers and possible identities beyond your belief. With it, you can control the future with nothing more than a thought. Or perhaps you will choose to battle injustice in one of its many forms. Maybe you are only interested in the more simple powers. Venture forth and we shall see.

THE CAPE OF GOOD HOPE

When you hear the word "SuperHero," what images come to mind? Can you remember the first time you learned of the concept? When I first learned of the term I could only imagine a Superman, or a Batman… some cape or another effortlessly sky-gliding to foil plots and save the day. It wasn't until someone characterized Jason Bourne (a character in a movie), jumping from one rooftop to another, running incredible distances, beating-up bad guys and still looking great for the ladies, as a SuperHero. In the past I called it escapism, movie magic, or even just another action flick. It wasn't until that moment, however, that my perception changed.

So I opened my mind, expanded my definition, and finally came to the same conclusion kids all over the world already knew: SuperHeroes are everywhere. They are embedded into the fabric of our very existence so deeply that sometimes we don't even notice them, and by the way, that's a good thing. Especially if you consider that even the very idea of a SuperHero can inspire us to fight injustice wherever we may find it.

Just don't fall in to the idea that, because they are everywhere, we now have permission to sit back and let someone else handle all of our problems for us. Instead, use this opportunity to become one yourself, and grow into a new, more powerful you.

Let's delve a little deeper to see where this takes us.

The first premise is that by recognizing SuperHeroes, we recognize ourselves… and not just the mundane personage that we have become, but our true selves. We can then take that discovery and live to our new potential.

In this book, SuperHeroes have been divided into three groups. This is by no means exhaustive but does provide a simple categorization that will help us not only choose who it is we wish to become, but also help us to choose our power base. Wonder what that means? Don't worry… it's about to be made clear.

So how does this book work? Well, it is meant to be a manual for turning the average (and even the below average) person into something amazing. This is not just A manual. It is THE manual. Yes, that's right: the one that turns mere mortals into the shining and supreme, God-like versions of the people they once were.

Most of the concepts you will understand just from reading the table of contents; others will get further explained in their respective chapters. Truth be told, this is way more fun when we just jump in and explore them. Actual hands-on creation beats the hell out of reviewing the syllabus any day.

One thing to understand about the layout of this book is that there are four parts. The first part is to help you understand exactly what it means to become a SuperHero. It will also help you to design your own SuperHero (not a fictional one… a real one—you!). Once you have that concept down, you will be ready for Part II: the extensive training of an exclusive SuperHero Boot Camp. It involves physical exercise and meditation and believe me, it's important. Part III is where the real fun happens: choosing your super-powers! Finally, Part IV is the aftermath. Questions like: "What now?" or "Where do I go from here?" will be answered in this, the final section. Sound like fun? It will be because at the end you get an official certificate of completion! Just kidding; you actually become a SuperHero (secret certificate sold separately).

Now, to be clear: On its own, this book will not make you a SuperHero. Only you have that ability. Your only prerequisite for this is simple: follow-through. That's it.

So there it is. Let's give it a go! You promise to try a little harder than you have in the past and maybe see what comes of it, and I promise to keep you entertained and maybe, just maybe, redefine your entire perception of things. Better yet, don't just try… actually do! And even better still… just be.

Why is this book so important? Because Captain America, in antithesis of Tinker Bell, died because we did not believe. His death was designed by Marvel comics, amidst events reminiscent of the Patriot Act. We, as a country, no longer believed in the concepts for which he stood, and that's a shame. We had lost ourselves, our understanding and our clarity. The world had become an enemy where bad things happen in the dead of night instead of an exciting adventure that beckons to the child in us. We didn't know where to go or what to think. In this time of moral ambiguity and crisis, the World absolutely needs heroes… The World absolutely needs you.

HOW TO BECOME A SUPERHERO

SuperHero DNA
A FIRST LOOK AT WHAT MAKES A SUPERHERO

A First Look at What Makes a SuperHero

What makes someone a SuperHero? A quick look at this chapter will illustrate things like: how to define a hero, a little about their history, heroes from around the world and in the movies, and then finally, make the distinction between hero and SuperHero. As an added bonus this is where you get to commit yourself to becoming a SuperHero. Ready? Then let's begin our quest and we'll start… with a little unmasking.

THE SUPERHERO SECRET

Just who is a SuperHero? Who qualifies and who does not? Would Superman be considered a SuperHero? Certainly it seems that he would. After all Superman can fly, he has x-ray vision (among other things) and is practically indestructible. If you're thinking that this was an easy one, then you're right. Heck, he's even got the word 'Super' right in the name.

Now what about Batman? He doesn't fly, isn't indestructible and doesn't even have a lot of the other, traditionally-defined super powers. In fact, Batman isn't even from some other planet like Superman or born of the Gods like Hercules or Thor. He's just a normal guy who spent fifteen years training his mind and body after his parents were killed. This being the case, does he qualify? Well, not to be flippant, but he does have a cape. He also performs selfless acts of heroism every day in the battle for truth and justice, and he certainly has a plethora of gadgets.

Let's make this more challenging, shall we? Let's take an ordinary man and give him a disability. Let's take away the most primary of all senses, the one most of us take for and see what happens. Let's make him blind. Other than that, maybe we can let him be in good physical shape. Is he a SuperHero now? According to Marvel Comics and almost everyone familiar with the story: yes, Daredevil, an above-average guy in an average setting, is clearly defined as a SuperHero.

So gadgets, abilities, the passion to stand up for something you believe and perhaps a desire to be the best… but what else does it take? Does it take a SuperHero identity or perhaps a costume? Surely this can't be it. Well dear reader, do not fret. There is one final ingredient… one even more important item we must examine. It is the greatest secret known to the universe, and it has remained hidden simply because it has always been in our plain sight.

It is only this: Ascension. Ascension will allow you to become the master of all you survey. Without ascension, however, you simply will not exist as a SuperHero. It is the deep secret that all SuperHeroes hold. It is this that gives them their great power.

What is this mysterious trait, and more importantly, how does it help to create a Super-Hero? In all cases of ascension (from Buddha to The Batman and from Jesus to Jubilee), each individual was called not merely to rise up, but to clearly rise above all surrounding humanity. There are those in our history, and even alive today, that rose above all others in ways that defied not only the odds, but sometimes even logic. Ben Underwood, for example had both eyes removed when he was three. Today, as a teenager, he uses echo-location to walk, run, play basketball, and even to play video games and Rollerblade. Yes, you read that correctly: echo-location. Like a dolphin, or a bat, he communicates with his environment through a series of clicks that help him to navigate. He can perceive his surroundings based on how the sound of his clicks bounces off various objects around him. With the exception of the cardio and gymnastic routines of the Daredevil character, the two might be considered equals—provided that you understand that one of them is a cartoon image and the other a real person.

Now, before I continue, allow me to wrap up this one point: Batman and Daredevil absolutely had all of the elements needed: desire, intention, action, a mythos, training, you name it. But most importantly, they also had that push that sent them from this world into the next. Batman is motivated by the double killing of his parents; Daredevil similarly is motivated by his father's murder. In response, they both chose to ascend to the next level of the evolutionary chain and this is what absolutely makes them SuperHeroes.

Ben Underwood has an incredible ability and yes you could even call it a super power if you wish. But he isn't a full-fledged SuperHero. That would take a real commitment to the cause. Now, this is partly because he does not have a mission; his powers are not directed towards any specific purpose. It isn't a far leap to imagine a simple mission that would work here though. What about spreading the idea of using echo-location to other blind youth, making them more independent, teaching them to be free, the way he is free. The choice to be a SuperHero is perhaps one he had not yet considered. To be clear, however, it is a personal choice, as you will soon come to understand, and it is not for everyone.

THE RISE AND FALL

Let's take a second here to cover how important the ascendancy is in order to claim your exalted status. It is in fact the only consistent requirement across all heroes and across all cultures… each one (from the Gods of Greek Mythology to the characters in the Matrix Trilogy) has ascended in one form or another. Without ascension, the hero does not exist. It is absolutely essential to rise above your fellow man in order to become a hero, and it is almost exactly what the word SuperHero itself has come to imply.

Once at this level though, even a hero can ascend further still. In fact, this is how the first SuperHeroes were created. They came from the ranks of the original comic book heroes back in the 1930's and 40's (more on this in a minute). The essential point here though is to never stop learning or growing; never stop striving to achieve. Even great heroes can achieve more.

This rising above the crowd becomes so important, and takes such a central role, that if one were to lose that accomplishment, or were to even temporarily devolve in some way, they would immediately lose their SuperHero status. It has happened to more than a few of the long-standing SuperHeroes of our time, either at their own request (Superman, The Thing, and Spider-Man, for example, were each conflicted and wanted to return to their past) or due to an extraneous mechanism (as in the development of Mutant cures in X-men, or the Neuralizer in Men In Black). As we can see, achieving SuperHero status is not at all an irreversible process. For the most part, however, those that have elected to become SuperHeroes originally, have usually decided to remain that way.

The moral of this story is basically this: In the case of SuperHeroes, and especially in the case of this book, the average are certainly encouraged to apply, but if you do, don't expect to be staying average for long, because that just won't work in the SuperHero world. That cliché you hear in the movies, when the voice-over says "A Hero will Rise" is almost correct. The full truth is not that a Hero *will* rise, but that a Hero *must* rise.

THE RISEN

Now, let us continue on with our supposed unmasking of the SuperHero and find out whom else currently makes the cut. Moving through our list, away from Superman, Batman, and the entire comic book subculture (Wonder Woman, Iron man, etc.), brings us to Gods and Demigods. With those like Thor or Hercules (or any of the heroes of different regions), this becomes fairly self-explanatory. Are they, themselves, SuperHeroes? Well, they are powerful, they have ascended, and they help humanity. As a SuperHero it would break down this way: the first two on the list (powerful, ascended) being the Super part, the last one (helping humanity) the Hero part. Quite often they also have a quest... and we will come to that topic soon.

Moving now along the spectrum one notch we have the characters typified by a Jason Bourne or a James Bond... or perhaps even the Heroes of Olde, like King Arthur, or Beowulf. They are all certainly amazing, but are they SuperHeroes? If they are, what about those like them; others that are at this level of power? Well, let us apply our SuperHero litmus test once again. What do they do? They unceasingly fight for a cause. How do they do it? With everything in their power. Are they far and away above the common man? Trick question. They are because they have ascended... but certainly anyone can follow their example.

The action heroes of the movies have the mythos, the gear, the training, and of course, the defining event that propels them upward and brings them safely down again, into the forefront of our lives (well ascended yet hardly ever well-integrated). Therefore, I give you this list:

★ **James Bond:** SuperHero.

★ **Maximus (from the movie Gladiator):** SuperHero.

★ **Hancock:** SuperHero.

★ **J.K. Rowling's Harry Potter, Hermione, and even Ron:** yep, you guessed it, all SuperHeroes.

Now, continuing our investigation again: further along our charts we have Fire Fighters, Policemen, Military (or anyone that risks their lives to save others every single day). Are they considered SuperHeroes? Well, let's categorize. As opposed to the cartoons and myths we have just covered, this group is real; here with us every day. These people can sometimes be labeled SuperHeroes… but they aren't all, and they aren't always. But this is by their choosing.

Some are missing a component or two. It's different for each person, and believe me, many of them certainly do qualify; many of them are absolutely SuperHeroes. But there are also those who don't measure up. There are average people, and then there are amazing people. The SuperHero is amazing. It's dead simple.

The goal here is not to denigrate, these groups as a whole are amazing. But we can do better than what we have allowed ourselves to accept. Another way to look at it is this: whatever you choose to do, if your intention is to elevate yourself to the level of the SuperHero, to truly ascend, then you must do it to the best of your ability, rise above the average, and become extraordinary.

Now that we have moved on to considering real people as SuperHeroes, I want to take a minute to discuss the Real Life Super Hero (RLSH) Movement. These are people that have taken on an alter-ego; they have a mission; and sometimes have even made themselves a costume. This puts them ahead of the game because they have already begun their upward journey.

An RLSH is a person making a difference in the world around them. I commend them for that. And I appreciate them for that as well. If more of us followed that example the world would be a better place. We all know that heroes and crime-fighters are a much-needed part of any society and that makes the RLSH movement an excellent start… To make the leap from hero to SuperHero though, they still need that one remaining element: the ever-elusive ascension. The best part about the RLSH however, is that for many of them that last step is the only step they need.

One that I admire in particular is Citizen Prime, an RLSH from Arizona. Citizen Prime himself will admit that he has probably stopped very little crime while out on patrol (but since not all SuperHeroes are crime-fighters this isn't really an issue). What he does have are ideals and he seems committed to them. He has also founded the League of Citizen Heroes with the intent of convincing anyone that they can become a SuperHero. His mission of spreading this idea may be far more valuable to him in his quest to become a SuperHero, than any time spent patrolling the streets. And when he is ready to ascend, I know that he will.

Here is another story of a real-life SuperHero, though she isn't a part of the RLSH movement per se. Her name is Alexis Jones and though you may not have heard of her, she is already making an impact on the world around us.

Alexis' SuperHero story actually begins a couple of years back. Picture our bright, starry-eyed Alexis, sitting in a classroom on her way to earning a Master's degree in Communications Management. As she listens to a lecture on Reality TV and the impact it has on society, we see the proverbial light bulb go on, and she smiles. Quite clearly, she smiles. Later that day she approaches the instructor with an idea and she says something like this:

> *"So what you're saying is that all I have to do is get on a Reality show... last long enough to be remembered, and then my message, whatever that message is, can better reach the world?"*

Short Answer: Yes.

Longer answer: Some disbelief and a little bit of that same response we give a child who tells us they want to be an astronaut. Sure honey, go be an astronaut. That'll be great.

So where does she go from there? She becomes a competitor on Survivor: Micronesia, almost wins the entire thing, and then goes on to founding a successful woman's empowerment group called "i am that girl" (IATG) in Los Angeles, CA.

Was it easy? Yes. Absolutely easy; especially if by easy you mean suffering a 104 fever, falling 25 feet off a cliff and blowing out your knee. Oh and did I mention how she got selected in the first place? Because that was easy too!

Somehow (and we still don't know how she did it), she found the secret date, time, and location of the final cast selection and began her journey. From there she managed to sneak past security, bluff her way past the receptionist, interrupt the selectee meeting and say "You're either going to arrest me or cast me, but here is why you should cast me." That takes courage.

Why did she not give up? What kept her going? She knew what she wanted and she simply did not stop until she got it. In her own words she says,

> *"I just kept thinking things like: 'Don't get voted off! —IATG, IATG, IATG— Last longer! You have to last longer.'"*

When she finally did get voted off she had somewhere close to 67 interviews scheduled, and what did she do with them? She spun every one of them into an interview about IATG. She laughs now that, "the media was not prepared for the smart girl to be at the other end of that microphone." It ended up launching her speaking career and gave IATG just the right spin in the media... and today? Well today they are a company in full swing and have launched programs in Cambodia, Ecuador, and even here in the United States. The moral of the story: keep your focus, hold on to your dreams, and for God's sake get out there and do something with them!

Moving on to normal people with normal jobs we again ask the question: Are they Super-Heroes? What about parents? Well yes, parents absolutely can be SuperHeroes but many of them aren't. They just don't make the grade.

In general, parents need to set higher goals. This is not to say that parenting isn't a mighty task—believe me, it is—especially if you want to do it right. What I am saying here is that many people seem to strive to get away with the bare minimum effort needed to raise a child, and in no way is this book, or even this concept, about being average. This also illustrates that a job doesn't need to be especially difficult for a person to be a SuperHero. You just have to be amazing.

In Las Vegas, for example, I watched a bartender captivate a bar full of people because of the way he juggled bottles of alcohol and mixed drinks with poise and flair. Of all the bartenders present, he was the only one who took that extra step. He took his job to the next level and did not accept entry-level behavior. He wasn't a SuperHero of course, but he did show the potential by refusing to be average in a place that would have welcomed the average. If you can rise above the others who simply accept their mediocrity, then you absolutely must.

What defines those who stand out? Whether we are talking about incredible athletes, charismatic actors, wonderful musicians, or powerful Greek Gods—why do we lift up certain people in our culture? Why Bob Marley? Why Michael Jordan? Why even Helen Keller? What is it that we cheer, if not the evolution (or perhaps revolution) of the Human Spirit? When you see them perform, you see them transcend the average capability and it touches you. It inspires you. It resonates within you because you know that you are capable of attaining that excellence as well. You watch and you know that there is hope for humanity. You absolutely know that one day everything will be okay... that it will all turn out all right, because if there is hope for them, there is hope for you.

If the thoughts presented here have intrigued or even frustrated you, then welcome, you are in the right place.

THE FALLEN

Now before you get the idea that all of the people portrayed here have to be above all reproach and live some sort of flawless existence, I should point out that this is not at all the case. In fact many of today's comic book heroes are popular because of their morally ambiguous choices, not in spite of them. For some it is the reality of their checkered past that attracts us to their character. This quality makes them not only more believable as characters, but also more accessible, because if they can find reprieve, so can we. As we talk about some examples, it is also interesting to see just how normal they actually are, even in some cases having regular day-jobs.

The Fantastic Four, for example, worked out of an office in New York City, having gone into the SuperHero business. Unlike Superman, who worked for a newspaper as a cover for his alter-ego Clark Kent, they chose to not even have secret identities. They chose "SuperHero" as a profession. Conversely, Peter Parker (aka Spider-Man) took pictures of his own exploits and sold them to the Daily Bugle in order to pay the bills. By looking at their reasoning, and also their exploits, you can begin to figure out where you fit.

As part of the general SuperHero growth in the 1960's the new stars of comic books revealed even more complex personalities and faced even greater challenges to surmount. It was an exciting time for fans and readers because it helped them to see the SuperHero as a real person; someone who had problems like they had; someone to whom they could relate. These SuperHeroes were also different in that they themselves were created in a more realistic way. It wasn't just their problems that were reality-based, it was their entire persona. Spider-Man for example, was just a 15 year old kid who liked science—talk about making someone more accessible.

What this does, in effect, is to open up the entire SuperHero field to the common man. If flaws are not the problem, if their past is not the problem, if even their age is not a problem… then this can only leave either the lack of understanding or the lack of action in commitment to the outcome. Let these stories be your guide. There need be nothing holding you back. In fact the only thing that does hold you back… is you.

The problems that you may perceive as overwhelming can actually be the very catalysts that spring you into action. Take for example the death of your parents (Elektra, Batman, and Daredevil). In these cases at least, the children were spurred into action. Or perhaps you feel that you have some personality disorder. Look at The Incredible Hulk, a flawed character that faced serious issues of self-loathing. Clearly not comfortable with his identity, he constantly struggled with his alter-ego Bruce Banner to the point of annihilation. And although our psyche innately sees The Hulk as just a demonstration of our ability for destruction—that immature, violent, child that people can sometimes contain—The Incredible Hulk is still an extremely powerful being in our culture. This is because he turned around what was once a limiting aspect of himself to bring about a greater good.

Comics weren't the only place that the terminally flawed found solace. The mythological Hercules killed his wife and children, and was thus called by the oracle at Delphi to perform a series of twelve seemingly impossible tasks that he may redeem himself… and even he became a hero. But remember, he killed his family! What this shows us is that ascension is powerful enough to help almost anyone start anew. The knight Lancelot was King Arthur's favorite by far, but had an affair with Arthur's wife Guinevere. Beowulf, who because of his ego, was always in pursuit of greater fame, was eventually killed pursuing it; he became a mighty hero nonetheless.

SuperHeroes have flaws; those of today as well as those of the past. It is what makes them likable, because in them, we can see a little bit of ourselves. Fictional SuperHeroes resonate with people because they are so clearly created in our likeness, flaws and all. What is most important however is not that these heroes are flawed, but that they are still able to perform such amazing feats. For this we will look up to them, while sometimes overlooking their little "imperfections."

> **❝ There are average people, and then there are amazing people. The SuperHero is amazing. It's dead simple.**

Daredevil, as just one example, has an alter-ego career as a defense attorney. Because of this, after he foils a crime, he will sometimes defend the criminal in court in order to cover his overhead and expenses. In fact once he even remarked that he needs to take it easy on street thugs lest he be out of a job (Daredevil #22, 1966). He has also, on occasion, resorted to questionable tactics to accomplish the larger good. To some extent though, this led to his downfall. Wonder Woman has the same story. She had decades of good service to her credit until one day she chose to kill a person to accomplish her goal. To many people, this was her downfall (Superman: Sacrifice. DC).

To restate the point, today's society would sometimes seem to instruct you that only the flawless have value. This is clearly not the case. There are stories, both real and imagined, of those who are not so physically perfect who overcame odds so great they would have caused even the able-bodied to succumb. In life it was Ben Underwood (mentioned above), or Oscar "Oz" Pistorius, dubbed "the fastest man on no legs," or sometimes referred to simply as "Blade Runner." Oz has taken his supposed handicap and become such an accomplished runner that he may soon compete in the upcoming Olympics. True to form however, the lowly common man is contesting his right to participate because of fear of an unfair advantage. As if somehow having no legs, and then making the best of it, is an unfair advantage. [*Editor's Note: He did not compete.]

In comics we would surely find a good example of this in Tony Stark, also known as Iron Man. Stark stepped on a landmine and so, continually on the brink of death, he must always rely on his iron suit (complete with a pacemaker) to keep him alive. If this weren't enough… he soon became an alcoholic and was forced to walk the long road of recovery. He hit the bottom; ending up homeless for a time, but eventually rebounded and was able to continue being the hero that many have grown to love.

Iron Man, like Oscar Pistorius, gives us the possibility of transformation, because underneath the suit Stark is a frail, dying man. It shows us that, if you need to, you can use gadgets, or strength, or even hope to help you become a SuperHero, no matter who you are. Yes he was an alcoholic, yes he was wounded in the war, and yes, he was flawed, but anyone, even you, can use the path of becoming a SuperHero to combat your problems. You must only want it enough to follow through.

If it is true that, often, there is something to be learned from our myths and our histories, be they Greek, Roman or even Norse, and if our comic books continue the collective stories that we tell our children, then these stories have served the purpose of perpetuating cultural values. If this is so, and these stories are rife with the common man rising to become an amazing, incredible hero, then the question to really ask yourself is this: If SuperHeroes are based on everyday people, sharing our flaws, yet becoming truly magnificent, then what is stopping you from doing the same? What keeps you from rising to become a SuperHero? Why have you not yet ascended? Why do you continue to hold yourself back?

FROM HEROES TO SUPERHEROES AND THE POP-CULTURE JUMP

The common man is a story you already know, so let's move past that concept. To do this we need to orient ourselves in the terminology of the coursework. Let's start with a definition of hero: "Characters that, in the face of danger and adversity or from a position of weakness, display courage and the will for self-sacrifice, that is, heroism, for some greater good, originally of martial courage or excellence but extended to more general moral excellence" (Wikipedia). Ok, sure, hero: yes... many of us have done that.

So what's a SuperHero then? Well, take your first definition and add the concepts we have been talking about: ascension, not accepting the average and pushing the limits of what you can accomplish. Throw in some helpful accessories, maybe a smidgen of some preternatural (or even supernatural) powers, give yourself a quest... shake well and presto: SuperHero!

In the same way it is interesting to hear about the general creation of heroes in the American comic book world, and then to watch their later transition into SuperHeroes as well; so here is a quick mention. The original comic book heroes were crime fighters. They handled bad guys with the greatest of ease; they were basically like intensified police detectives. Around the time that comic book heroes were coming into their own, World War II (also coming into its own) happened to be drawing us ever closer.

This change in the world matched the environment that was painted in our comics. It was a great, coming evil. It swept up the innocent. It called for a hero to come to its rescue. As a country, America was that rescue. In a sense, we were that hero. Our comic book heroes of the time reflected this change to our consciousness. The writers and artists began sending our heroes to war in the comic books as well.

Captain America punched Hitler in the face. Batman and Robin handed out rifles (and when Batman planted himself behind a machine gun, Robin helped to feed him the ammo), Superman sold war bonds and stamps. Everyone, it seemed, got in on the action. After the war was over, our heroes, fresh from fighting the evil Axis powers (i.e. the world's greatest villains), couldn't just return to simply fighting muggers. They needed new tasks and new challenges. They needed to grow, as did our country. They, in turn, left crime-fighting behind and started to battle ever-larger creatures in their quest to yet again keep the world safe from a global harm. As SuperHeroes they grew. As people they grew. Now it's your turn.

PUT IT IN WRITING

Remember in the beginning of the chapter when I mentioned that this is the part of the book where you get to become a SuperHero? You didn't forget did you? I hope not, because this marks the beginning of a wonderful change in your life. The idea of commitment is so important that I have devised a short contract for you to read and sign. Don't worry, there are no hidden clauses here, but you are definitely signing away your life. You are signing away your average life, that is!

I, _____ , pledge to undertake this task of becoming a SuperHero. I understand this will require me to complete the exercises in each chapter with great attention to detail. I will put great care into designing every part of my SuperHero persona and in return, be rewarded with everything I want for my future self.

Signed _____

Date _____

All done? I hope you are excited. Now, before you move on to Chapter two and learn to see the future, there is just one more thing you must do. E-mail your contract to us at Contact@ SuperHeroPress.com. This will be the beginning of your journey. We cannot wait to hear about all of those that are now on their way to becoming SuperHeroes. It will solidify things for you. It will make it real. When I joined a competition to write a book in 30 days, it did not become real to me until day 3, when I signed the contract and posted it on my wall. It was all the motivation I needed: my own word. I hope this will be just as powerful for you.

Through The Haze

A FIRST LOOK AT SEEING THE FUTURE

A First Look at Seeing the Future

What if you had the power to not only see the future, but also to change it? Intriguing isn't it? Better yet: What if you could just create everything as you saw fit? Teaching you to do exactly that is my goal for this chapter as we move you from simply reading about the SuperHeroes of the past and onto becoming one of the greatest SuperHeroes of our time.

Why would you want to see the future in the first place? Well for one thing, it makes life easier. Isn't it much simpler getting somewhere when you already know where you are going? Doesn't it give you a much higher chance at success than if you didn't know?

Another reason to see—and in fact create—the future is the joy of commitment. If you know where you are going, you can commit to the journey. This is very powerful. Having the chance to commit to something bigger than yourself can be extremely rewarding and very fulfilling.

So where the last chapter showed you the history and helped you see that anyone can become a SuperHero, this one shows you how to use your own inner abilities to do so yourself. In it you will be given all of the mental tips, tools, and skills you will need in order to reach this goal. Also, you will be shown how to ascend. This will not be some unrevealed secret, at which I only hint. Instead the steps will be clearly laid out in front of you. You, of course, will still have to walk them.

By the way, it is important to point out here that this chapter contains most of the mental components necessary to become a SuperHero. Don't worry. It isn't ridiculously difficult; you will only need a few things: vision, commitment, and ascension. Each one leads to the next one in the list (including ascension, as it points back to the new level of your vision).

While you are learning to see and create your own future, you will also learn how to (really, truly, and fully) commit to something. You will need that in order to actually become a SuperHero. You will also need to learn how to ascend. Without this chapter nothing can be accomplished in your SuperHero journey. With it, everything else is a snap. Are you ready? Let's begin.

What do we know about SuperHeroes? Well, starting from the beginning, we know that they must have an origin, right? It makes sense... I mean everything else has one. We know that someone or something drove them to become what they are today—even if it was only themselves.

Now of course traditionally this was a traumatic event (i.e. a death in the family, a planet exploding, great emotional stress, chemical spill, what have you). We also know that this event changed that individual forever. The person who experienced that traumatic event becomes the SuperHero. It's a tried and true formula.

What they do not become—and I cannot stress this enough—are victims. Let me give you an example: When you run into a SuperHero, do you hear them always whining about their past or their problems? Um, hello? No… you don't. No matter what disaster they were solving just before you got to the restaurant, they do not spend the next half hour of your lunch date re-hashing it at you. Nor, may I remind you, are they busy telling you for the tenth time about that rough upbringing they had. That's what victims do, and SuperHeroes are definitely not victims.

Ok… what does this mean for you? This means that if you are to be a SuperHero, then you must stop letting the events of your life (and the people around you) always push your buttons. You must take control. It must be you; not the person next to you, not your dear aunt Sally, you. You can take control of your future, and responsibility for your past, any time you choose.

Let's try a concept or two to help send that idea home: Yesterday is not today. Almost every mere mortal reading this book right now believes that it is. Think about it. When you wake up in the morning, first thing, bright and early, what starts? Your routine. Bam! Gotcha already.

But let's take this a little slower to make sense of it. I am not suggesting you live a life of chaos. I understand that your routine has probably evolved over a long period of time, and for good reason, right? But it is there… day in and day out… Starting to see the rut?

But the idea of "yesterday is not today" extends to more than just being in a rut. What are you holding on to as if you were still stuck in it? From what unfortunate event, or bad situation do you refuse to be free? Think of the freedom you can bring yourself by simply letting go. If yesterday is not today then do yourself a favor and stop living it again and again. You had it once, now celebrate it and move on.

Let's look at another branch of this concept. Many people will tell you that your past experiences make you who you are. This is not true. Your past does not make you who you are. It makes you who you were. Only you decide who you are today and who you will be.

I ask you, if you met a career accountant who had already spent 5 years in the cubicle job that was his life, certainly you might think his schooling and his past created that role. You might spend 2 years watching him, and feel that your supposition was correct. But what happens when he suddenly walks out of his office, never to return, and joins Greenpeace in order to save whales? Day 1 in the raft and he has no idea how to handle the situation in front of him. In that moment his past did not determine who he was or what he did.

A CEO decides she has prepared her entire life for taking a company public but then decides to inexplicably retire and move to the country… An amnesiac awakens and knows not who they were, but instead chooses who they are… You are what you decide. No more, no less. If a person's past truly did decide their lot, then we would all be slaves to our past and to our mistakes. We would have no freedom to choose our own direction in life. We could not will ourselves to change careers or even jobs. We could not change. Period.

Yet we know from experience that we can change. We can decide. Our past history therefore obviously does not make us who we are. Only we have that power. This means that every morning, and in fact every minute, we can have a clean slate if we so choose. A tabula rasa in every pot and a fresh start in every driveway!

So now that you know it's possible, how do you actually get away from it all and start fresh? Well, for that you have to wake up. Simple enough, but just for clarity, let's walk through it. Have you ever heard of highway hypnosis? It's when everything in your life starts to look the same and it lulls you into a trance. You go on auto-pilot. If that isn't the life you want for yourself, then snap out of it!

But wait—aren't we supposed to be seeing the future right now? Good question; but first things first. You can't see your way to a better future without clear vision, and to paraphrase Anaïs Nin, "We don't see things as they are, we see things as we are." This means that you have to break free from your past and from your old habits in order to see something new. And besides, the best way to predict the future is to create it. If you see it clearly enough, right now in your mind, the rest of this book will teach you how to get it. However—and this is a big however—you will never, I repeat never, accomplish it with your old behavior.

That isn't a judgment about how far you have come or what you have accomplished. It simply means that whatever thinking it was that got you to the point you are at now, is not going to help you become a SuperHero. What got you there will not get you here. New action equals new results. Realize that first. For example, take a look at your current peer group: Can they help you become a SuperHero? Understand what a fresh start really means... then move on to the next section. And don't worry, after this chapter you will be able to see clearly enough to see your future (provided you follow the advice). Then, throughout the rest of the book, I will help you develop your grand vision for it.

WHAT YOU WRITE, YOU ABSOLUTELY CREATE

Now that you're ready to part with your illusions of the past, and have a desire to see your future clearly, I ask you: Where is the future created? It is created right here, right now. How does it come to be so? Simple: we decided it. We decided it before, in the yesterdays of our lives, and we decide it now, in order to beget all of our tomorrows. If this is a new concept for you, look at it this way: your decisions, not someone else's, have brought you to exactly where you are, here, today. If you realize that each new choice can lead in a new direction, then this becomes a powerful force for change. Let's explore this a little more, shall we?

It is important to understand that you are the only author of your future. Only you. This means that if you write a possibility today, you will create that reality tomorrow (barring one particular exception of course, which I will explain below). As such, I should point out that this book has a mission: to offer you a chance at becoming more. It is designed to make you want something… to dream about it, and finally, to create it.

In a word, what I am offering you is this: everything. You will see a world of your own design; a reality that behaves as you dictate. This is an opportunity and it is waiting for you, that you may become the ideal for which you have always ached. Surpass those who do not undertake their own upward journey. You will find your own existence irrevocably changed for the better. You have seen it in the movies, heard about it in the folklore and mythology, and even read it in all the popular fiction of the day. It is on television and in all of your conversations. Every story is one of growing, defeating and overcoming. Do this in your own life. Own the idea that you will become the hero that saves the day. You can become—you must become—the SuperHero!

There is a leap of faith required here, and honestly it is the only one required in the entire book. You are being asked to believe that the future you want is absolutely achievable, with your own work and dedication. That's it. Believe in yourself and the power of your choices and you will arrive at your desired (and totally amazing) location.

> **❝ You can take control of your future, and responsibility for your past, any time you choose.**

I will point out here that the SuperHero metaphor is only one way to create that future. As the saying goes, there are many paths up the mountain. Now certainly, this way is the most fun (I mean, seriously, who wouldn't want to be a SuperHero?). But provided you have the strength of your conviction, and can act with follow-through, you will accomplish your goals, regardless of the method.

Let's bring this section to a close with a simple question. Do you absolutely believe that with enough time and effort, even if you don't actually know how yet, that you have the power to create any future for yourself that you choose? Any future, bar none? Is it at least theoretically possible? Here's an example to help solidify your answer.

If you are a painter and you have before you two people to paint who are standing side-by-side, perhaps a homeless person on the right, and Donald Trump on the left, does it not take exactly the same amount of skill and effort to paint both likenesses? That is to say, whether you are painting guy left, or guy right, are you not still expending the same amount of energy, effort and skill? Clearly you are. Painting one will use the same process as the other. Your detail in what you create will still be there. You will be just as exacting.

Life works the same way. Donald Trump is the world's foremost expert on becoming Donald

Trump. He can tell you how he got there, what he did, what he does everyday, etc. He can show you better than anyone else the story of his life. But the same is true for the homeless guy. If you were to emulate exactly all of the movements of either person for 10 years, you would become as they have become.

Yes, it might be difficult. But do you now understand that with the proper focus, and enough of your energy, that you can absolutely become anything you choose? This includes becoming a SuperHero. You will need a couple of special tools here however, and that's ok because you already own the book. The tools have already begun to shape things for you and they will continue to do so for as long as you actively choose.

Whew! We are finally done with that section. The question now is, if you really can write any future you choose, then where and how do you start? You start by controlling yourself.

CONTROL YOURSELF

Who is the best person to determine the outcome of your life? This is the part where you resoundingly say: "I am." Well, if you want it to be you who decides the future of your life, make sure that you are up to the job. That is to say, if you want to be a SuperHero, you must stop giving away all of your power and your responsibility. More specifically, you must pledge to stop allowing others to take unconscious control over you. Please read this one more time, and more slowly: "Stop allowing others to take unconscious control over you." Notice the word unconscious here. Yes, you absolutely may want to stop others from taking any sort of control over you, but what are we saying by unconscious control? Acting unconsciously means you are acting without direction, without thought, without consideration. Throw away the idea of hindsight. It only means you weren't paying attention the first time.

Let's start with the opposite. It may be more valuable for you to first understand what it means to become fully conscious. This is a supremely powerful SuperHero ability and will appropriately be discussed several times in this book. To be conscious is to connect to everything, to see potential in everything, to allow everything to come together and to be in control of this process. To be in the flow. Sound difficult? Only if you say it is!

If you are conscious you are attuned to everything around you. You are conscious if each of your actions has a complete purpose to it simply because you are aware of them. But it is also much more than this, and this next part is key. Consciousness is being awake to the idea that your mind creates everything: from the relationship you're in, to the heart attack that could cost you your life. When you understand that you are truly this powerful, that you have created all of this through your own free will, you will begin to design the world as you see fit. I could stop the book right here and if you could but grasp it you would need nothing further.

Once you learn of the power of consciousness, you will begin to understand the true detriment of not living it. You must understand: you really can design a life in any way you see fit. More to the point, you already have. The life you have is the life you made. Each detail was hand-crafted by you. When you become conscious, when these things are as natural to you as breathing, then you will create your masterpiece.

Also, there is only consciousness and unconsciousness. When you are acting unconsciously, you do not take responsibility for your actions, or your future. You are not acting from a place of power or with intent. Consequently, you unknowingly give your power away to everyone around you. You are asleep, and the people that take this power from you are asleep as well. No one that is asleep can take care of you, or ensure the future that you want for yourself. As a result, you become a victim of circumstance, and it is then, when you will shake your fists at the sky and wonder how such a thing can be so. But the answer is that it never has to be. The answer... is that you must wake up! Wake up to your life, and wake up to your power.

If you have followed the steps up to this point you now realize that you are free to write a new role for yourself; in this case the role of the SuperHero. You can vaguely see the outline ahead of you and you probably understand the need to create it consciously. Before we start creating however, let's take a look at your ability to fully commit to something. You will need this to ascend, and you are about to learn it right now. One interesting way of learning to fully commit is by analyzing a scene from a movie.

Let us go now then, as in myth and the movies, and visit the Oracle that we may benefit from rich wisdom. Let us see what the future has in store and give ourselves the life we seek. Whatever it is, if you create it, will you follow it? Will you fully commit to it? Do you even know how? Or will you remain the hapless victim? The choice is yours but you do have the power to consciously create it. Do so, and you will create magnificence.

A VISIT TO THE ORACLE

In the movie <u>The Matrix</u> (Warner Bros. Pictures, 1999), the character Neo has a visit with the Oracle. Once there, he receives amazing points of advice. Most notably, these four:

⇨ **1** SELF-KNOWLEDGE IS A TREMENDOUS POWER;

⇨ **2** YOU ABSOLUTELY HAVE TO BELIEVE;

⇨ **3** YOU ABSOLUTELY HAVE TO ACT; AND FINALLY

⇨ **4** IT CAN ONLY BE YOUR IMPETUS, NO ONE ELSE'S.

The four statements above are deeper than they look, so let's examine each one more closely. By the time we are finished with all of this, however, you will be able to dedicate yourself completely to any task.

The Oracle's 'Advice Point One': Know Thyself. Self-Knowledge is a tremendous power. Without it, according to Sun-Tzu, you will lose every battle. Your biggest battle in becoming a SuperHero will be with yourself, so win this battle first.

On that note, how much do you really know about yourself? Do you even know who or what you are? If I may for a moment paraphrase philosopher de Chardin, "you are not a human being having a spiritual experience, but instead you are a spiritual being having a human experience."

Think about that for a moment. Imagine yourself, right now, as an all-powerful, spiritual being. Breathe deeply and think about that: You are all-powerful. How do you feel in response? Does your chest expand just a little perhaps? Now this time, imagine that you are just a small, ordinary person again. Imagine that you no longer have any supreme power. Do you notice a difference in your posture? Maybe even a difference in thought?

What I am saying is simple. If you knew that you were all-powerful, truly all-powerful, would that change you? If so, how? What would happen if you believed that you were far greater than just your physical body? What if you were so much more in fact, that the capabilities of your physical body would pale in comparison to those of your mind and spirit? What if you, the person reading this right now, became the shining ray of light that would illuminate any path? What if you had the power in you right now to stand bold and strong, and were able to walk any road you chose? In part, this is the life of a SuperHero. Take from this that the possibility of yourself, your true self, is limitless.

Believe that there is something inside of you that can rise above. To do so is to celebrate the power contained in us all. Commit to building and becoming the SuperHero. Hold on to the power you felt when you considered yourself an all-powerful being. It is our perceptions that define our reality. And that perception you had, of feeling all-powerful, is completely important to your SuperHero training and to the reality you will soon create.

You can become a SuperHero, and if you agree to it, you will become a SuperHero. If this were not true, then you would not have found this book. If this were not true, you wouldn't be on the verge of becoming more powerful than you ever thought possible.

Wow! All of that from the line: "Know Thyself." It rather makes me wonder what's next.

Let us move now to **The Oracle's 'Advice Point Two'**, namely, you absolutely have to believe. Believe in the power to be conscious, believe in your own power to become supreme. In The Matrix movie (continuing our discussion from above) the question of belief was asked numerous times by many characters. Belief was central to their mission.

In fact, in the movie it was as if no one could move forward without first having that knowledge in hand. Morpheus asked Neo to believe, and then he asked Trinity if she believed; Cypher asked Trinity, Tank talked about it, the Oracle had gobs of it; and towards the end even the Agents had a case of the Beliefs.

All of this brings us to one central point. Your dreams will absolutely fail without your fully-committed support. This includes the idea of becoming a SuperHero. It almost seems silly to have a dream and to not believe in it, and yet, millions of people do it every single day. Ask yourself: if you're not going to believe in them anyway, why dream?

The next lesson from the movie, relative to this section, is that once you have a dream, according to **The Oracle's 'Advice Point Three'**, you must now act on it. Obvious yes, but you can be sure that millions of dreamers will never take that next step. You cant just imagine your way to a better future. Belief is not enough. It is important, it's true, but if you stop at just believing then nothing will happen. A belief is only lip-service to an ideal. You believe because you don't want a concept to die, but you must act on it for it to really live.

Let's try it this way: As I mentioned before, in the movie everything began with belief, but then progressed upwards from there. When you read below, notice how things increase from step to step.

➡ **STEP 1:** "Morpheus believes he is the One." (Trinity to Cypher).

All of the characters are asked whether or not they believe. In this stage, belief was the only thing that was judged in a character. If they had it, they were validated (Morpheus, Trinity, Neo). If they didn't, they were vilified (Cypher). Then, later on in the movie, belief is no longer enough.

➡ **STEP 2:** "Don't think you are, know you are." (Morpheus to Neo).

This illustrates the need for greater commitment in our thoughts. In this stage it is no longer enough to only think or believe. Now we must know, with conviction, that we are an incredible manifestation of our own design. There is no turning back, you either know it in your heart and soul (or from "balls to bones" as the Oracle says), or you fail. You must choose whether you simply believe, or whether you truly know. And clearly, the stakes are high. Next:

➡ **STEP 3:** "There is a difference between knowing the path and walking the path." (Morpheus to Neo)

Ok, this progression is huge and has been said in different ways from Dante to Niemöller. Just knowing a thing, means nothing if you never act on it. There is a world out there that will never benefit from, or even learn of, your gifts if you refuse to act. If what you know, goes no farther than your own mind, what was the point of gaining that knowledge in the first place? Does it matter that you think something is wrong, unjust, or in need of change, if you never speak up?

As an aside, there is another popular movie that draws a parallel here: Batman Begins (Warner Bros. Pictures, 2005). In it, the character Rachel Dawes tells Bruce Wayne that "it's not who you are underneath... it's what you do that defines you." Don't just leave an idea in your head and don't just believe in something; act on it.

Having understood action we now move to the next phase of our character's journey.

➡ **STEP 4:** At the end of The Matrix, the character Neo no longer walks the path; he just is (the one).

And here, in this section's final point, we find out that even when you act on something, it usually isn't enough. I know, I know. It's crazy right? First you are believing, then knowing, then they've got you actually doing something, and now... now they tell you that one action is just not enough. They must be crazy. Every person who just kept going, and just kept doing more must have been crazy. Each time somebody made their life about a cause or gave everything they had in order to stand for justice, yes, they were crazy. Absolutely and completely crazy. There are some in this world who lived and died to achieve their vision. You have the power to accomplish yours without the need to become a martyr. There is a way. This... is that way.

If you want to accomplish something, just make it who you are. Be it in everything you do. I guarantee you that you will become that champion. Gandhi did not say to just "do the change you want to see in the world."... he said be it. After all we are human beings, not human doings. You must embrace it and must become it; with everything that you are.

All of the world's greatest heroes have understood the difference between just performing an isolated action and actually giving everything they had for a cause. SuperHeroes don't just try to fix something... they fly into action with such resolve and passion, that by this alone they often succeed. They fully become it.

Sometimes too many words are used to explain the simple.

BELIEVE ➡ KNOW ➡ DO ➡ BE

These are the four steps; this is the process of true commitment. When you truly commit, you will be ready to ascend. The steps are simple, but they are not easy.

What is it in your life that deserves this sort of commitment? What speaks to you, drives you, incites passion? What is so powerful for you that you would dedicate your life to it?

....

....

**When I talk about commitment I am literally talking about making your entire life about this one thing.
WILL YOU RISE?**

At the end of our visit to the oracle we have **The Oracle's 'Advice Point Four'**: the impetus. Your actions cannot be for someone else. Your journey has to be of your own accord. Using the words of Morpheus one final time: "I can only show you the door. You have to walk through it." You will be glad you did.

You have just crossed the threshold into your future. If you have grasped Chapter 2 you will fully understand commitment to something.

When this power of focus is gained you will understand what you must do to ascend —to truly ascend.

The future is within your reach now but it is raw and unformed. In the Bhagavad Gita it says that there is great power in the un-manifested.

Come with me —venture forth!

You will soon learn how to shape it as you desire. You have many more tools coming.

Makes and Models

A FIRST LOOK AT THE HERO TYPE

A First Look at the Hero Type

You have just overcome an incredible hurdle. Already your power is increasing. You may not yet know it… but your world is being reshaped around you.

Your future will evolve and then appear just as you choose.

Have you ever wanted something so badly that you absolutely would not rest until you had it? Whatever the item, the experience, or even the person… you said to yourself that you simply must have it (or them)? If you felt it—I mean really felt it burning in your veins, it is probably safe to say that by now, you have accomplished, achieved, or had it.

One relatively unknown, yet supremely accurate, fact of life is that "at the very moment we decide that we have no other choice but to make it… we achieve our goals." It is that clearly stated need to make it to the other end of the swimming pool. Without that need, you will not make it. With that need, you will not be stopped. It would seriously take ending your life to keep you from it. You know what happens next? You make it!

In the simplest terms, what did you do? You aimed. Hopefully you can see now that, as mere mortals, we sometimes have our own clear-cut goals and we do not rest until we reach them. The SuperHero is no different. Their goals and desires are just clearer and more frequent. By the way, that part about a SuperHero's desires being more frequent should not be taken too lightly. In a funny way, a SuperHero is supremely self-centered. Think about it: more than any of us, they have a desire to impose their will upon the world. Granted it has been to our overall benefit (otherwise they would be a Super Villain), but they do it none-the-less.

Now before we cover those goals and desires, which (for clarity's sake) are presented in a separate chapter, let's talk about one of your goals as a mere mortal: your goal to become a SuperHero. We already know that SuperHeroes can come from anywhere and that they can also begin as anyone. Well obviously, if they can be anyone they can also be you. Did you think that maybe you weren't the type? What if I said that you were exactly the type it took to become a SuperHero? What then? Well then you would have to choose what type of SuperHero you want to be!

So now I challenge you to take the next step. Jump off that cliff, from the safety of where you now stand, and become the SuperHero you have always wanted to be.

I dare you.

INTRODUCING THREE TYPES OF SUPERHEROES

Choosing your SuperHero type will be the primary choice you make in Part I of this book. Later on you will add other elements to complete your SuperHero identity: things like powers, a mission statement, even a symbol. You may use this book (and your new identity) to become a SuperHero in any aspect of your life; to accomplish whatever you desire. It isn't only about fighting crime. Becoming a SuperHero means to be empowered to create life as you see fit.

To guide you, there are three different categories. It is important to mention that this isn't about a hierarchy of SuperHeroes. It is simply a means to an end. All significant paths have both opportunities and challenges. Also, since every new SuperHero must complete their Core Training in SuperHero Boot Camp, you can be sure that everyone will have the same level of competence (depending on their level of commitment) by the time they finish.

You will choose your SuperHero type based on what is important to you and what you want to achieve in life. Perhaps you will even combine or re-work certain categories to fit you better, or even make your own. This is mostly just a tool to better understand your own, inner SuperHero.

As you read on, you will be pushed to determine every aspect of your SuperHero self, down to the most minute detail. Imagine it like a funnel. Right now you are at the wide part of the funnel. It's easy to jump in—there's lots of room. But as you get deeper into the book, you will be pushed more. You will define every part of your SuperHero identity and you will do so with confidence!

The spout of the funnel, however, (and this is the coolest part) is individually shaped. You get to design and craft it to be whatever you want. And when you emerge, provided that you have followed all the steps, not only will you be a SuperHero, but you will be ready for action as well! Remember: the greater the detail of your design, the more complete will be your reality, and consequently, the more you will achieve. Ok, ready? Then jump!

➡ FREELANCER
UNIFYING YOUR MISSION WITH YOUR JOB

To become a Freelancer is to become the SuperHero of your occupation. Whether you are a student or a construction worker, there is someplace where you ply your trade. Once there, the Freelancer transforms into elegant, moving perfection. The Freelancer achieves excellence in these endeavors simply because they have decided that this will be their area of focus. They make it who they are.

It of course draws its name from the idea of freelance work, and as such, has some real-world roots. In the mortal world, a freelancer usually has one very developed skill, or set of skills, which they bring to various companies in need of their help. Their life's focus is more about honing that one particular skill or niche, and less about just working for any one particular company. Common examples include graphic designers, artists, writers, and hit-men. They have the freedom to decide for whom they will work, and when, and can more easily direct their own agenda with this freedom.

This SuperHero category then, is characterized by not only being very focused on a particular task, or skill (like your job perhaps), but by then merging that with your SuperHero mission. In later chapters you will understand more about your mission, but for now just realize that as a SuperHero you will definitely have one, and being a Freelancer, this will revolve around your job.

Is there a part of your current job to which you can bring complete focus and grace? Maybe you have an outside passion that you would rather see transformed into your career? Or perhaps you want to integrate your outside interests with that of your current job? For the Freelancer at least one of these carries a resounding "Yes." For some people the "9-5" has negative connotations; not so for the Freelancer. Remember: The SuperHero sees possibility in everything.

So whether you want to become an outstanding parent, a superior employee at your job, or even the world's best student, the Freelancer category is your fast-track for getting there. Like the mere mortal version of the Freelancer, you are focused on your best skill, using it at different times, in different contexts. You are so good at what you do, that it instantly transforms anyone who comes into contact with it—like the bartender mentioned in Chapter One who was so incredible. Your audience is always irrevocably changed… transformed by your mastery.

If I am at work, I have a particular mantra that I like to use to inspire me to the level of a Freelancer. The first line I even borrowed from Kwame on season one of the The Apprentice. It goes like this:

I have had my entire life to be ordinary. I now have
this one moment in which to be extraordinary.

I will perform this one act so completely, so incredibly, that my ac-
tions here today will resonate for eternity and will absolutely inspire
this person to be the very best they can be in everything they do.

All of my focus, here, in this one moment, on this
one person, will be absolutely amazing.

And then I serve that person in any way that I can. This is just one way to elevate your mindset to that level. I have saved this phrase to my cell phone and will read it out loud, verbatim, until I am in the frame of mind I choose for excellence.

Perhaps an example of a real-life Freelancer-type SuperHero will help you better understand this category. Let us consider the example of Tiger Woods, and his father, Earl. Now you might think that Tiger is the SuperHero of this story. Well my friends… that is not the case. The real SuperHero here, and the shining example for the world, is his father Earl.

Earl Woods started bringing his son to the golf course with him when Tiger was only two years old. Now, I certainly applaud the father-son time, but all good stories have a twist and this one is no differ-ent. The unexpected result of these outings was that his son Tiger became a child prodigy at golf by the time he was three. Stop for a minute: three. That's right... Tiger was only three, yet completely amazing.

> **Whether you want to become an outstanding parent, a superior employee, or the world's best student, the Freelancer is your fast-track for getting there.**

Earl Woods did an incredible job of parenting. It was not only his mission, but also his means of bettering his part of the world. What does that make him, you ask? Ka-bam! Super-Hero; specifically: a Freelancer. He easily fits into the Freelancer cat-egory for his fantastic parenting skills. He even wrote two books on the sub-ject. Now seriously... what have you helped your child do? Those of you that have accomplished the incredible with your children understand exactly what I am asking the others.

To share just a little: I have two children and Earl outperformed me easily. It isn't that I have failed, per se... only that I am not a SuperHero parent. This was Earl's gift and his target... he worked to perfect his skill. And he nailed it. I think it's fantastic. As the rapper DMX puts it: "We each have a star, all you have to do is find it. Once you do, everyone who sees it will be blinded."

Earl Woods set his son up for success; he offered Tiger the ability to succeed at something that he (Earl) already enjoyed, and something in which he could guide his son. Earl didn't only teach his son golf however, he taught him how to succeed at a thing completely. While this is a great skill for the sporting world, it has great value outside the arena as well, and Earl helped Tiger learn to do just that.

If you look at where Tiger is today, you can understand the outstanding work of his father as a Freelancer-type SuperHero. It might even make you think that Tiger Woods has himself become of the Freelancer-type SuperHero, albeit in the sport of golf, as opposed to parent-ing. Well, you're almost right.

He did master the sport. Tiger Woods is consistently ranked as one of the top players of the world (if not the top). He was also the highest paid professional athlete in 2006 including his endorsements and winnings, and he is also predicted to be the first billionaire athlete by 2010. This example does rival SuperHero performance, it's true... but somewhere towards the end of the example we can see that Tiger misses the mark.

Yes he is amazing at his job (golf), just like a Freelancer would be. But being a SuperHero takes more than just being good at your job. Tiger had no great mission for bettering the world. Once you have that, you must integrate it into your life. His father looked outside of himself to see where he could most benefit others, and chose his child.

As are all SuperHeroes, Earl was the servant-leader. He chose his son to serve and then poured in all of his focus. Tiger doesn't do that. Although, in his defense, he didn't say he was a SuperHero. He said he was an amazing golfer. And he certainly is that and more.

➡ FREE-RUNNER
UNIFYING YOUR MISSION WITH GREAT PHYSICAL PROWESS

This category is named after the sport of Free-Running (similar to Parkour). Free-Running is a sport that shows off physical agility and training using a combination of gymnastics, acrobatics, and coordination. It is often done in an urban setting, utilizing normal parts of the city landscape as obstacles to surmount. Free-Running is practiced for show, while Parkour is aimed at the most efficient and practical way to traverse any terrain. The movements in both are very similar, however, and it is often hard to distinguish the difference just by quick observation.

You may even be familiar with certain elements of these sports, even if you don't know it! One example would be those movie chase scenes where you see physical limits being challenged (and in fact sometimes re-written or even erased). If you have ever seen shots of people jumping across rooftops, swinging from balconies, jumping to the ground from incredible distances, you have seen performances of Free-Running and Parkour.

This SuperHero type, then, is designed for people who desire to increase their physical ability; to push the limits of what is humanly possible. To become a SuperHero in this category is to model a character like a Jason Bourne or the Batman. What do you want your body to do? Of what do you want it to be capable? While this will help to lay out the main focus of your training, this does not, in and of itself, make you a SuperHero. You still have to define your goals, and you'll need a mission as well (just like in the Freelancer category above). Start thinking about that now because soon you will add all of those elements.

As above, so below. Since our last category had a real-life example, so too will this one. A really great example of the Free-Runner-type SuperHero was Raymond Belle. You may not have heard of him... but there are a great many that have, and more than a few who owe him their lives.

He had such great courage and physical ability that he became a military firefighter in Paris while still just a teenager. He absolutely excelled; rising quickly to the elite sector of that regiment. Not only did he stand out with his superior athleticism, but his devotion and courage were such that he was often called upon to undertake the most dangerous missions. His reputation soon grew. As word spread of him being such a self-sacrificing, skillful firefighter, he continued his efforts and went on to earn many accolades and medals. Belle dedicated his life to his mission of saving others and developing his own physical ability. His work as a firefighter, and his amazing athletic prowess was so great, that he inspired his son David Belle and David's friend Sebastien Foucan to go on to become founders of the sports of Parkour and Free-Running (respectively). Because it is hard to explain to you just how incredible these sports actually are, you may want to search the Internet, or look on YouTube, to really get their full impact.

Raymond Belle saved many people. He inspired generations. He was physically superior, and he had a mission to save lives and help and inspire those around him. All of the things that made him a SuperHero are things that are within your reach as well. If this is the type of SuperHero you choose to be, it is only a matter of beginning your movement—literally, your physical movement. Get up... now, and do something, anything. Begin simply, but you must still begin. Remember, we still have to add in your mission, and that is coming... but you do not have to wait for that chapter. In fact you must not wait. You must rise.

➡ FLYER
UNIFYING YOUR MISSION WITH GREAT MENTAL, SPIRITUAL, OR PSYCHIC POWER

This last category is for those that are most focused on the development of powers that many would consider otherworldly. Their powers are at a level of which they see no obstacles in anything they do. Fictional examples include Neo, Harry Potter, or the Silver Surfer. As was discussed in chapter 2, Neo was only able to succeed at things when he finally knew he could. It was not his physical ability that helped him succeed. He failed at first because he wasn't sure if he could do it, he didn't believe, and he didn't really know who he was.

SuperHeroes in general see no limits; and will accept no possibility of failure. Add to this the fact that SuperHeroes are so committed to their goals, that they would absolutely give their lives to see them accomplished, and some of them have (to varying degrees). Real life examples are Nelson Mandela, Gandhi and Mother Theresa. They saw no limits, because really there are no limits. More on this last point later, but for now, let's not get ahead of ourselves.

As mentioned, Mandela, Gandhi, and Mother Theresa are SuperHeroes, but they're not Flyers; they're Freelancers (they dedicated their lives to their work). If you are surprised by this and wonder something like: "Wow, if not them, then who does qualify as a Flyer?" remember, this isn't a hierarchy. It is only a path.

Having said that, the Flyer takes all of the initial requirements of the SuperHero and then elevates them even higher, so as to become an art form. In the comic book world compare Batman to someone like the Silver Surfer. A solid glimpse at the unrivaled ability of the Surfer might send Batman back to the cave to reconsider the meaning of true power. On the other hand Batman is in the trenches every single day accomplishing his life's work while many see the Silver Surfer simply as aloof, uncaring, and sometimes (even physically) distant. Which SuperHero does more good?

These are the things that keep this from being a contest of "who's a more important Super-Hero." There are different walks of life and different values to be upheld. There is no shame in being good at your job, and potentially tremendous fame and success for being amazing at it; just look at Michael Jordan! It's all about what you like; what you choose to support.

As we discussed, the type of SuperHero you choose has a lot to do with the powers you most want to develop. Knowing this, where might we find a real-life example of a Flyer for you to study? For this we must look for someone who has spent their entire life cultivating supreme mental, spiritual or psychic power. Before I tell you, remember: although you may not always see the practical output of a Flyer, they are still important because they remind us to challenge the limits we put on ourselves every day. Even though these limits are self-imposed, this doesn't stop us from creating them. If we stopped imposing limits on ourselves completely, we would no longer have the need to be merely human. We would simply ascend. Stop placing limits on yourself and you too can grow to become this (or any) type of SuperHero.

As a Flyer you will always surmount your obstacles, no matter what they are (provided you don't get stuck in your head). Flyers are the real proof of limitless power in our world. So who then is our real-life example? Well, even though he was called "The Man Who Invented the Twentieth Century" you may not have ever heard of him. In the early 1900's he invented or helped to further the development of:

*THE FLUORESCENT LIGHT

* SEISMOLOGY

* A WORLDWIDE DATA COMMUNICATIONS NETWORK

* THE INDUCTION MOTOR

* THE RADIO

* WIRELESS ENERGY TRANSMISSION (SENDING POWER THROUGH THE AIR WITHOUT CORDS)

* THE SPARK PLUG

* A RADIO CONTROLLED BOAT

* EARLY ROBOTICS

* A/C POWER

* ARTIFICIAL LIGHTNING BOLTS OF UP TO 135 FEET IN LENGTH

* EXTRACTING FREE ENERGY AND POWER FROM THE AIR AROUND US

* **AIRCRAFT THAT TAKE-OFF AND LAND VERTICALLY (WITH NO NEED FOR A LANDING STRIP)**
* **A COSMIC RAY "DIRECTED-ENERGY" WEAPON**

He had a photographic memory and made his first million when he was 40 (and in 1896 that was something). He then went on to rip up a contract that would have made him the world's first billionaire, because he didn't want to restrict his own plans for the future. Instead he moved forward to live a great, yet very dramatic, life, dying penniless and alone in a hotel room. Talk about choosing your own destiny! His name was Nikola Tesla. He worked for Edison and Westinghouse, helping to pioneer both, and had all of his plans and documents confiscated by the FBI.

The true power of a Flyer comes from developing their internal ability (be it through Mind or Soul), and you must understand that there simply is no way to fail. This is the heart of things. As a Flyer you have the power to literally reshape the world. Does this sound crazy? I promise you, it is the truth, and if you will but truly commit, you will have the power you so obviously desire.

DECIDING ON YOUR SUPERHERO TYPE

You have now read about all three categories. Still not sure in which category you belong? If you don't feel like you fit into one category perfectly, you can play with them a bit and combine them to fit your own goals. No one is a purist. Mix colors from different pallets and what you end up with the most, well, that's where you end up. Also, within each category we do have room for distinctions and different personalities.

For example, in the preceding section we talked about Gandhi and Mother Theresa and we suggested that they were Freelancers. Clearly a case can be made that their ability came from God (though their ideas of God may differ). To view them in this light then we might say that all they did was to work on improving their own spiritual connection and then allowing that manifestation to flow into the world around them. Well... that's a Flyer. Is it a contradiction? No. It's a viewpoint.

Another good example is a martial artist. Assume that he is very advanced physically and has a mission to educate the world about his art and to improve their way of life. Per our examples then, he is a Free-Runner. Now say he opens a Dojo and uses his business to accomplish that same mission, and we might more easily see him as Freelancer. If he also has an advanced sense of Qi and works to improve that internal power, you could easily call him a Flyer.

I didn't make this up to prove my point. The example was based on Darren Levine. He is a well-known martial artist, a successful entrepreneur, and an even more successful prosecutor for the Los Angeles County District Attorney's office (he has a 100% conviction rate). At one point he was the highest ranking Krav Maga instructor in the United States, with 6 training centers and thousands of students. He holds fast to his ideals and works hard on each of his missions.

Don't get caught-up in the details. Remember, choosing your SuperHero type is only the beginning. I say this because it doesn't limit your choice of Super Powers later on. In Part II you will be able to select powers from any category you choose. Choosing a type right now is only a guide to help you focus your mind for the future. In other words you can absolutely choose to become a Free-Runner because you like the physicality of it, but then add the powers of a Flyer later on as well. Remember: This is all about designing every detail of your life, the way you want it to be.

Another option, if you're not sure which category to pick, is to go back to the "Answer the Call" exercise in the beginning of the book. Take it seriously and really consider what is inside you. Sit back, close your eyes and imagine being called to action.

This will start your process of narrowing everything down. Remember you are only in the wide part of the funnel, so the easiest thing to do now is just to JUMP IN! When you are ready, complete the box below. Just don't go past it until you have decided.

Yet another way to choose your ideal SuperHero type is what I call "The Jimmy Stewart." Actors are called upon to play many roles and to become many people. Jimmy Stewart said, "I played a role once that was Jimmy Stewart, and people liked it so much that I just kept playing it." Some people have referred to this as "Fake it till you make it," but I disagree. I think that not being your best in life is faking it.

What it really means is that you must decide who your ideal, greatest self is (the one who always acts so coolly in every situation), and then you start being that person immediately. Said differently: if you were your own highest ideal, and you wanted something done right, who would you call? Yourself!

One of the founding principles of this book is the idea of becoming your absolute best.

What this means is simple, but please read these next 3 sentences very slowly. If you are faced with a difficult solution, don't ask yourself what Superman would do, ask yourself what you would do if you were there. Not just you as you are now, but your highest self, your best-case scenario, the absolutely ideal you, the you that you really want to be. What would you do if you were there?

So how does this relate to our current discussion? Well if you haven't yet been able to choose your SuperHero type, this is just another method with which to do so. What type of SuperHero do you wish that you were? In your perfect world, which one would you be? Answer this... and you are ready to move on to the next step.

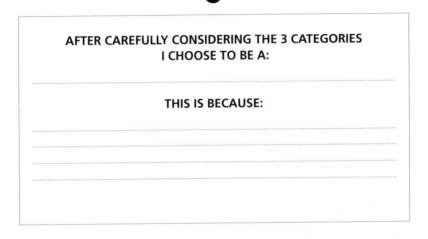

**AFTER CAREFULLY CONSIDERING THE 3 CATEGORIES
I CHOOSE TO BE A:**

....

THIS IS BECAUSE:

....
....
....
....

Are You a Good Witch, or a Bad Witch?

A FIRST LOOK AT THE GOOD, THE BAD, AND THE MORALLY UGLY

A First Look at the Good, the Bad, and the Morally Ugly

Your journey has now clearly begun. You have a guidebook. You have decided on your level of commitment to this process, and you hopefully now have decided which type of SuperHero suits you the best. You don't yet have your mission, or even any fancy, new powers... but they are coming soon.

Before you can choose a mission however, it must be decided whether you will serve the forces of Good, or the forces of Evil. If this decision seems obvious to you, perhaps you should read on in order to see the full picture. You may find the true answer to be anything but obvious.

Which will you choose to become: villain or hero? Do you envision yourself the champion of justice? Or perhaps the dark terror that rises up for retribution? And curiously, do you even know the difference? Choose carefully, brave soul, as things are not always as they appear.

In either case—SuperHero or Super-Villain—your course shall remain basically the same. You will be given the opportunity to learn, to study with the others, even to ascend to that greatest of levels I know you so studiously seek. With effort, focus, and diligence, you shall achieve your coveted status.

This book is not here to judge. That is a task I leave only to you. You *will* however be taught how to look beyond the surface in order to see the impostors of Good and Evil as they truly are. It is not requested that you apply this vision to others... only that you look deep within yourself. Once there, you will have the clarity that most will forever lack.

Strip away your preconceived notions and journey inward. With patience you will find your inner Truth... and consequently, your power of Vision.

DEFINING YOUR MORAL CODE —THE EVIL THAT MEN DO

Let us begin with the easy questions: When is it right to kill? When should a person take another human life? Or perhaps even the lives of many? Does the greater good exist? In this chapter we will be talking about morality, but not as you may have ever seen it. Could it really be that this book would advocate for a mere mortal to become a Super-Villain, as opposed to a SuperHero? Is there value in ascension (the prime requisite for becoming a SuperHero) regardless of the outcome? Unraveling these questions in your own mind will take a further bit of reading and perhaps even a mild dose of introspection.

In Chapter 2, specifically in the section about commitment, we learned that being a Super-Hero calls for action. Fluidity of action stems from clarity of vision. Only when you see the situation clearly, will you be able to act with impunity. Therefore, to see things clearly we must first do away with your preconceived notions.

Going back, then, to a lesson we learned in that chapter: What is it that keeps us from seeing clearly? It is only ourselves. More specifically, and please read this next bit slowly, it is all of our knowledge that keeps us from learning. Think of it this way: when you know something you basically categorize it. You put it in a mental box, and stick it on a shelf somewhere in your mind. If you *know* it, you no longer have reason to study it, to learn about it, to question. Because you know it... you stop looking at it with fresh eyes.

I hope I am never *known* by anyone. Think about it: you aren't free to change. They *know* you. What does that even mean, anyway? How can you hope to gain the totality of someone's great existence from just a few casual meetings?

In fact, how many times have you, yourself said "Oh, yeah... I know that guy."? You know what he's about, of what he's capable, and just what his angle is, I'm sure. He is a closed case to you. Am I to be labeled and put on a shelf? No thank you, I'd rather get off at the next stop.

But seriously, can you see how that works? At least with people perhaps? Can you see how they might grow and change beyond what you think you know about them? The world around us is intensely big. How much can you really say you definitively know about anything?

Now, other than people, think of everything else that you know. Think of all the things that you are so sure that you know so well that you never have to be open to the possibilities they present ever again. These are biases. They are based on all of your past learning. The more preconceived notions you bring to the table, the more closed off you are. The more you *know*, therefore, the more you are stuck.

I started this chapter this way because you need to abandon the idea of judging and labeling others. You will not find it instructive. People are not inherently bad, nor are they inherently good. Trying to apply a simplistic label to a complete human being is ludicrous. More importantly it is childish, and the more you perceive the world through the lessons of your past, the more you will stay stuck in that reality.

So then if we are to abandon the idea of labels, why do we have a chapter on labeling our own morality? Because understanding your own motivations and methodologies is a valuable tool. We will use this chapter not to judge what others have done in the past, but only to further our own journey. Here's a question: As a SuperHero, if you saw a guy being chased by somebody, is he a criminal that you should stop, or a victim who needs help escaping? In the real world, one person's struggle *for* is always another person's struggle *against*.

Don't believe me? What about Christopher Columbus? Yes, in 1492, he sailed the ocean blue (as they teach you in school), but along the way he committed acts that were practically genocidal against the Arrowack tribe when he landed in what is now America. Yet, we still have a whole day celebrating his actions.

Or what about Indiana Jones: Is he a movie hero or just some guy stealing religious artifacts from indigenous peoples? Even more glaring, Nelson Mandela won the Nobel Peace Prize for his fight against Apartheid but was labeled a terrorist by those in South Africa who wanted to remain in power. To this day he still cannot enter the United States without a special waiver because of it. Was Nelson Mandela a terrorist or a Freedom-Fighter? History decides in retrospect; the SuperHero decides in the here and now.

In the land of comic books, Superman prevented Batman from reaching his mortal enemy the Joker because, at the time, the Joker had diplomatic immunity. Was he right or wrong? These examples are all designed to question your concepts of right and wrong. They are meant to be tricky. They are meant to be confusing, and they are NOT clear-cut.

The liberator of one country will sometimes be the oppressor of another. Even here in the United States, at our very beginning we had to fight, and kill, thousands of people in order to become sovereign. Did we make the right decision? Were our actions justified? Were the many deaths suffered on both sides worth it?

When you do eventually decide the truth for yourself, will you stand up and be its champion? Only you can know for sure. The real questions I am asking should be clear: Who are you? In what great concept do you believe? What will you do about it?

It is your job, the job of the ascended, to stand up for what you believe. To fight to uphold the concepts you love and to fight to oppose those that you cannot bear. You, the risen, must never fall into someone else's convictions. You are the strongest of our generation; our hope and our future. Carve out your direction from the barren rock before you. Rip it from the hands of those too weak to decide for themselves. But in all things, stand tall and stand strong with the courage to support your own indomitable will.

A SYSTEM OF MORALITY

Good, Bad, Up, Down. It isn't about judgment. It's about taking you to the next level. To do so, we need a system of morality. Something easy, that just spells everything out. Ok, how about Dungeons and Dragons? Go with me here for a second. In the game of Dungeons and Dragons, "alignment" is used to describe people's moral outlook. So then, at least in one way, it fits our purpose. That's good enough for me!

Remember: the reason we are using this system is not so that you can classify your enemy as either this, or that. Labeling others is a tool of the lazy; as such it is completely useless to you. This system is devised so that you can better understand your own actions and build your strategy from there. Morality is your framework and foundation. May it serve you well throughout your quest (For more info check out Wikipedia or the Complete Scoundrel

Sourcebook). Now on to the game!

All the players have basically nine choices for morality. This comes from two initial categories (*See Chart*). You pick one from each column and join them together (e.g. Lawful Good).

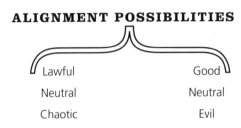

ALIGNMENT POSSIBILITIES

Lawful	Good
Neutral	Neutral
Chaotic	Evil

LAW/NEUTRALITY/CHAOS

Starting at the top of column one, we begin by describing Lawfulness. On the plus side we have traits like "honor, trustworthiness, reliability, obedience to authority" (Wikipedia), and respect for the rules of society. These are all pretty great things right? Well, although this seems like a straight shot, there are some downsides to Lawfulness as well.

A strict adherence to the rules can leave a person inflexible and closed-minded. You take Henry Ford, for example: if he went to lunch with you and you salted your food before you tasted it, he wouldn't hire you. He figured that meant you were stuck in your ways and not open to new things.

However, things like respecting the rules *can* help to create an environment where citizens can depend on each other and can establish a common understanding about the direction of that society. This is similar to John Locke's idea of a social contract. He believed that the general collection of opinions from the people must rule society. Lawfulness helps to create that and helps to peacefully lead society.

Next we look at Chaos. Sounds terrible, doesn't it? But believe it or not, Chaos actually provides many benefits—things like "complete freedom, adaptability, and flexibility" (Wikipedia). Perhaps it is only under these conditions that new ideas and personal freedom can truly develop. Let the free-thinking populace applaud. Chaos allows for a laissez-faire sort of culture. The best will rise, independent of the rules and structure of society. But of course, Chaos also leaves room for impudence, rebelling against authority, a lack of restraint, and irresponsibility.

This leaves us with Neutrality which, surprisingly, isn't just a bland mixing of the two, or even the best of both worlds without any of their negatives. It does, however, fall somewhere in between. Those of a neutral disposition show neither an innate honor, nor a dishonor, for the rules of society. But nor do they go out of their way to either respect or disrespect those rules.

It's interesting, isn't it? This is just Column One, and already many of our common perceptions have been challenged. Knowing the overall tone for which these alignments are aiming can be very helpful then in deciding a plan of action for the future. In other words, if you are the sort of SuperHero who is aiming for complete world freedom, or even the type that envisions a society that exists in a quiet peace, then by understanding these initial categories you will better understand with whom to align yourself and who you truly are as well. By the way, this gets really fun when you are choosing a SuperHero partner (in a later chapter, of course).

THE GOOD, THE NEUTRAL, THE EVIL

Now let's jump over to Column Two. The easiest way to explain these are with short, direct sentences. Afterwards, you will be shown complete examples from both the real and fictional worlds that will illustrate how different characters have used these alignments to successfully further their own ends. Picking a role-model among them may help you apply what feels most comfortable to you (especially after seeing the outcomes that they have obtained in their quests).

➡ **Good:** This quality refers to that of human compassion. They have a self-less concern for other human beings, and may even make personal sacrifices to come to the aid of others.

➡ **Neutral:** The neutral do not agree with killing the innocent but do not go out of their way to help others, either. The personal relationships that they are able to form are of their primary concern.

➡ **Evil:** In opposition to the quality of good, the evil are interested in causing hurt, taking the life of, and taking away the rights of, others. They lack human compassion and can act in such a manner without conscience. Some will actively pursue such activities.

Ok, so what does all of this mean? Well as I mentioned we have some sample combinations (and their outcomes) to show you below. It makes it all more tangible—especially with so many choices available to you. Read about them, then try to understand their implications as they would apply to your own endeavors. Whether they are from real life or popular fiction, you may find the results quite instructive in your own planning. Knowing who you are, as well as knowing your goals, will help you plan your alliances and better strategize your conquests.

THE ALIGNMENT COMBINATIONS

➡ **LAWFUL EVIL:**

Those interested in using the order of the law for their own means, regardless of the rights or interests of individuals. A good example would be dictators who have undertaken extreme uses of force against their people to maintain order (Think: Stalin, Hitler, Hussein).

➡ **NEUTRAL EVIL:**

People of this sort are utterly individualistic, and looking out only for themselves. They have no real connections to others and will use evil actions to get what they want. Examples include Jafaar from Disney's Aladdin and X-Men's Mystique.

➡ **CHAOTIC EVIL:**

Those that have a general disdain for the rules of society, and use evil to create disorder, panic and ruin. From fiction we have the eponymous Gremlin from the movies, and any sort of demon of the underworld that thrives on chaos and destruction.

➡ **LAWFUL GOOD:**

One who acts with compassion for others and upholds the rules of society. We often may think of chivalrous knights and paladins. Today, Boy Scouts of America may also come to mind.

It might seem obvious that a SuperHero would naturally be Lawful Good. This is not the case. Batman, in a famous encounter with an assassin called the Beast, helps to illustrate this point. After chasing him through the city from rooftop, to streets, to sewers, he finally has him cornered underground in a closed room. The Beast invites him to settle once and for all who among them is the best. Batman simply refuses and shuts the door... sealing the assassin in, presumably to die. Afterwards he remarks, "Sometimes you have to ignore the rules. Sometimes circumstances are such that the rules pervert justice. I'm not in this business to protect the rules. I serve justice." (Ten Nights of the Beast, Batman 420, June 1998).

Superman, on the other hand, is absolutely of Lawful Good alignment. He refuses to deviate from the rules of society. The best example of this was mentioned above where, in a Batman comic (Death in the Family), the Joker (Batman's enemy) was given Diplomatic Immunity because he was Iran's delegate to the United Nations. A CIA representative explained that basically this meant all the Joker's crimes (widespread murder included) were swept under the rug. Superman refused to allow Batman access to the Joker because, to him, that would have been wrong. So Batman punched him in the face.

➡ **NEUTRAL GOOD:**

A neutral good character is conscience-driven, and acts with compassion towards his fellow men for, or sometimes even against, Lawful precepts such as rules or tradition.

An example in today's world is Doctors Without Borders. On their website they say, "[The] decision to intervene in any country or crisis is based solely on an independent assessment of people's needs—not on political, economic, or religious interests. [Doctors Without Borders] does not take sides or intervene according to the demands of governments or warring parties." Simply put: laws are seemingly irrelevant to the goals of the organization. Thus if need be, they will absolutely do what it takes, including showing a disregard for politics and law to help the injured, the wounded, or the sick, even to the point of helping an enemy.

➡ CHAOTIC GOOD:

Those that act against the established rules and law in the name of protecting the rights, freedom and greater good of the people.

Fictional examples include Jack Bauer from 24, Disney's Mulan, and Robin Hood. In our real life we have people like Noam Chomsky, constantly disrupting ideas about established norms and laws, yet doing so for the common good. He rails against apathy and the status quo in his fight for a better future for all humanity. Also people like Thomas Jefferson or George Washington, who wanted to overthrow the government in favor of a better system, would fall into this category.

➡ LAWFUL NEUTRAL:

One who strongly adheres to the law but may often throw in their own, personal moral code as well. Since our legal system is based largely on interpretation, a judge is a great example of this category. They uphold the law above all else. Further, when it comes time to pass judgment, this person is absolutely prepared to pull the proverbial trigger. In fiction, James Bond would be a prime example. Also, being neutral to good and evil allows this type of person to kill when necessary. They are free to punish, take advantage of, or even cheat, another in order to maintain the laws that they are sworn to uphold.

➡ TRUE NEUTRAL:

Those that are neutral in all respects. Examples include people who are solely interested in keeping a balance, above all else. Some instances of this would be the actions of an animal conservationist who exterminates some animals, thinning the herd, in order to save them as a whole. Also, when a forest ranger does a controlled burn in one area, to save another area. In both examples, the actor is not against the animal or plant, but must kill in order to maintain a balance.

From fiction we have the Overlords from Childhood's End, (Sir Arthur C. Clarke). Rick from Casablanca (at the beginning anyway), and Switzerland (which is totally fictitious as I don't believe that such an idyllic place exists).

➡ CHAOTIC NEUTRAL:

Ranging from the up and happy, free-spirited person, to the downright nasty anarchist, a person of this alignment is surely an individualist. The chaotic neutral follows their own desires, discarding and disdaining rules and traditions. Freedom of action is probably the most important source of motivation here.

From fiction we have people like Snake (from the movie <u>Escape From New York</u>) or even Captain Jack Sparrow.

YOUR OWN ALIGNMENT

Now before you start wondering why this chapter was necessary, or why you needed to know about alignments anyway, consider this: understanding your true nature will help you seek out goals that are better aligned with what you truly want. Remember: passionately serving an ideal is the hallmark of the Super-powered, and knowing who you are helps you to more easily decide. On a more pragmatic level, you will have a much easier time constructing your mission statement, which is coming up next. And what does that mean? That you are one step closer to becoming the complete hero. One step closer to becoming... a SuperHero.

Done with the chapter and on to the exercise. Now that you have read, and hopefully understood, this short chapter on a constructed morality, you should begin thinking about your own alignment as a SuperHero.

⇨ **1** What values are important to you? How do they work together?

⇨ **2** Will you act out of self-interest? Will you act in the name of others?

⇨ **3** Are there any areas in which you refuse to choose a side? (This is dangerous.)

⇨ **4** Also, make sure you understand your own neutrality. This is different than refusing to make a decision (above). Neutrality in some areas allows for more freedom of action in others. It's what they mean when they say "Pick your battles."

⇨ **5** Finally, how would you label your own alignment?

Fill out the chart below to help you discover what your own alignment will be.

VALUES I UPHOLD	NEUTRAL	VALUES I OPPOSE

I CAN SUMMARIZE MY MORAL ALIGNMENT BY SAYING:

Congratulations! You made it through a rather arduous section. You may take a break if you like, but the rest of us are moving on with our journey. At this point you know what type of SuperHero you will be; you know that you can create whatever future you choose; and you even know your SuperHero alignment!

That is nice work, but still only theoretical. I mean, what will you do with all of this knowledge in the real world? Well, you are about to have a chance to figure all that out! Not only will you create a general vision of the future, but you will also choose your defining purpose as well. Why become a SuperHero? The answer is surely different from person to person. Let's take that reason and show the world! See you soon in Chapter 5.

The Road Less Traveled

A FIRST LOOK AT DEFINING YOUR MISSION AND VISION

A First Look at Defining Your Mission and Vision

You are now on the road for which you have been searching. It is this road, the one on which you now stand, that will take you in the direction of your dreams.

Take a look over there. You see that mountain off in the distance? Well this path you're on... this... road beneath your feet: this is how you get there. It is a road of heroes and there have been many a traveler.

If you make it to the base of that mountain, a pathway to the top will literally open up before you. When you reach the summit, I want you to turn around and face everything you have left behind. Call it a tribute, if you like.

When you do... when you see it all, so clearly for the first time... only then will you be able to jump—no, only then will you be able to leap. To soar high above all that you were. You will look down and see the roads that have brought you there. You will see the people who were your mentors and your guideposts along the way. When you see them, and you know for sure, I ask only: that you continue to fly.

To those of you that have not been completing the exercises, the readers taking a more passive approach, I implore you to go back. Now is your opportunity to return to the beginning and complete those exercises. You must understand that you are reaching the oft-fabled point of no return. Travel too far down this road without the proper tools and the road will be forever lost to you. This is not spouting doom or nay-saying. It isn't as if you'll die. I mean... you may... but not because of this. What I am saying is that this road will be forever lost to you.

Take me at my word here. At this moment you have the power of innocence and magic on your side. At this moment, you have a fresh start; the world is full of possibility. At this moment you don't even know what the rest of this book will say. For all you know, the rest of this book unlocks the hidden dimensions of reality known only to a select few. But this is exactly the point: you don't *know*. This book still has enormous, transformative power for you.

Once you do know what it says, you will either have opened those magic doors or you will have found that you don't have the key. It's a long journey, my friends. And I absolutely guarantee you that you won't make it twice.

So just bring that key with you now... one simple step, and you will have the comfort of knowing that you will succeed. Head back, do the exercises (actually write them this time), and we will wait for you here. I promise, the book won't progress any further until you are ready.

THE ROAD AHEAD

Ok. Everyone present and accounted for? Fantastic! Then let us now speak of this great road that lies ahead. A SuperHero is honestly something far greater than most of humanity can fathom. As such, those of you on the road with me today have traveled significantly farther than you may realize. Your commitment to this has been truly inspiring. As a small reward for that dedication, each of us have gained a few more tools to use in the shaping of our SuperHero selves. But the road isn't over yet. We still have a lot of ground to cover before nightfall, so grab your packs and let's get moving.

Now considering we spent the last few chapters with an eye to the past, cleaning up any messes and misconceptions we had along the way, let us now look to our future. In so doing, I bring you the section on creating both your Mission Statement, *and* your Vision Statement.

While they may not look like much on the surface, there is a power to be harnessed inside these two documents. Multi-national corporations have them. Successful presidents and world leaders have had them as well. The world of success thrives on clarity. These documents will help you focus your vision. They are a directive force that will help you hone your decision-making skills and lay open the path to your future as well. How will they do this? Let's start with the mission statement and figure that out.

> *"Creating a Personal Mission Statement will be, without question, one of the most powerful and significant things you will ever do to take leadership of your life."*
>
> —Stephen R. Covey

MISSION STATEMENT BASICS

In the general sense a mission statement is a document you write, that declares to the world why you are here; or... said differently: the reason you choose to exist. In our case the question would be more appropriately stated as why you choose to exist *as a SuperHero*. There had to be *some* reason you decided to answer the call, so start there.

Whether you wanted to make some great difference in the world, or perhaps even accomplish a specific task, your mission statement is the place where that gets written. The process is fairly simple: You determine it, flesh it out some, say it aloud a few times, and then (and this is crucial) shorten it. Ideally you are looking for one succinct, guiding sentence. Also, it should be so easy that a sixth-grader can understand it. Think you can accomplish that? If you've made it this far in your training, then I would say you can.

When you think you've got it, you have to memorize it. Memorizing it, along with writing it down in the first place, is important because it helps you to always have a place to go when you need it. When you find yourself looking back at your mission statement in the future for guidance and direction, you'll understand why this part was so important.

WHY HAVE A MISSION STATEMENT?

Well for starters, what if I told you that it was the measure of all your activities? It is; or at least, it should be. A well-designed mission statement helps you decide how to act, what to do, and even what to say, in any situation. This is pure truth. As a SuperHero your main function is to act in pursuit of your ideals. If you reflect the light from your mission statement onto all of your activities, you will instantly know whether or not you are on track to fulfilling that mission.

Why else might you want a mission statement? Because it can help answer tough questions. Issues like "why am I here," "what is my purpose," or "damn I just lost my job" are probably obvious, and yes, the mission statement will help answer them, but you're on the road to becoming a SuperHero, and yours will likely be different. What if the question is more like: "Does that person need my help?" If you can mentally get yourself to the point where you can judge your actions by how well they serve your mission, you will know the answer.

I'd like to point out that that last question was asked on purpose. The hardest lesson for the do-gooder to understand is that not everybody needs, or honestly even wants your help. Sorry... but it's true. Not only that, sometimes you can't help, while other times you just shouldn't help. Even if it looks bleak, and sometimes especially so, you have to avoid being drawn in. Let me use some examples to illustrate what I mean.

If you have ever witnessed the struggle of a butterfly trying to break free from its cocoon, you may have a better idea of what I am saying. In watching the butterfly break free, it seems sometimes as if the little guy won't be able to make it. Like maybe with just a little help, perhaps a quick tear here or there, everything will turn out right. But here's the trick: the butterfly needs that struggle in order to strengthen his wings for flight. Without it the butterfly dies. Said differently: if you interfere with that person's struggle, you may not actually be helping them... you may instead be hampering them.

Here's another example... if you over-water freshly-planted grass, then it never learns to reach down into the soil for its water. It thinks instead that water is always near the surface... easy to grab and utilize. Next time it needs it, the water may not be there. It dies because the first journey was too easy. It sounds contradictory, especially for a SuperHero... but sometimes the best thing you can do is let someone have their struggle.

Sounds confusing doesn't it? That's why a SuperHero needs clear vision. A mission statement clears part of this confusion away for you. One way it does this is by allowing you to focus on your strengths, and your chosen areas of life. There are many ways to help people. Use your strength; channel it through your mission statement.

Let's look at it from another angle. With our recent understanding of a constructed morality (in Chapter 4), you may find yourself wondering about good decisions vs. bad decisions. Here's an easy rule-of-thumb: Decisions that move you closer to your goals are good ones. Decisions that move you further away from them, are bad ones. It's that simple. But this can only help you if you know what those life goals are. Starting with your end goal in mind means you will have a directed way of getting there.

CHOOSING WHAT'S RIGHT FOR YOU

Time to dispense with the theory and move on to the action. We are to be SuperHeroes after all. In this section you will be taught different ways to actually construct your mission statement. In fact, you've been seeing subtle hints all along. To bring it into sharper focus you will be guided somewhat at first, and then also given a list of steps and suggestions for building something of which you can really be proud: A mission statement that strikes at the heart of who you truly are.

Before you get going here are some tips:

➡ Speak Strongly – Use SuperHero verbiage.

➡ Use the strongest verbiage you can during the construction of this document. Make it SuperHero language. Be bold. Speak as a SuperHero would. This is important because our words shape our reality. Use Super-Hero language—always.

➡ Mission statements are especially applicable to the SuperHero. Can you imagine Iron Man sitting at a coffee shop, just hoping something comes his way? Create it, then act on it.

➡ Remember to keep it brief (3 sentences at the most, but ideally 1-2), and keep it simple.

➡ Our goal here is to choose a mission that works for both your career and your personal life. Keep this in mind.

➡ A mission statement showcases the primary reason you exist.

➡ Keep it short and clear and use it everywhere (press releases, public addresses, etc...).

METHOD ONE – NAME IT AND CLAIM IT

This is basically like a free-writing exercise for those well-versed in who they are. If you're still stuck in your story don't use this one. My assumption here though is that, by now, you know mostly about who you are, where you're at, and what lies ahead of you.

This will be more true if you have been writing down and completing the exercises in this book as they came up. If you haven't been, then this method (the most powerful one) may not work for you. Jump down to the next one, instead.

For those of you that have been doing them, good job! You're about to make the rest of your life an amazing adventure. As an added bonus, in addition to becoming a SuperHero, you are also becoming a more conscious creator, and trust me... that's a good thing.

What I am telling you is that you now have the power to just make things what you want them to be. It is no more complicated than that. I will let you in on a little secret however: method one, the one I'm explaining now, is in fact the very method I myself have only just used (perhaps a few hours ago, in fact) to create my own mission statement. Seriously, for this method you just start writing and say that your mission will be whatever you say it will be. Watch the guidelines I gave you, yes, but just begin, and write it how you choose.

You may begin now, of course, though you may find it useful to read over the other methods in case you are looking for structure. They are great for that. Some of them will even provide you with templates. Good luck! Though I know you won't need it.

➡ **Step 1.** Start with what you already know about yourself.

➡ **Step 2.** Decide what you most want to be doing.

➡ **Step 3.** Describe who you most want to be.

These are not necessarily in order. This only helps you structure your free-write. Remember: aim to have the finished product be just one or two sentences.

As a final note on this method, since this was the one that I myself used... you may find it instructive to see my own personal notes on the subject. You don't have to read it... it's certainly not required. But if you're interested, here's basically how I did it. (PS, they're just personal notes... they're not designed to all make sense.)

WIKIPEDIA: BOATMAN-LIKE BODHISATTVA
One who aspires to achieve Buddha-hood along with other sentient beings

MY GENERAL THOUGHTS
To live the life of the SuperHero in all that I do; absolutely inspiring humanity to rise to their next level of existence through teaching, conversation, and writing.
A few sayings of mine, that I had liked from the past, and had myself oft-repeated, etc...

HERE'S AN INTERESTING NOTE ABOUT MY PROGRESS.
I took hours crafting something that I thought was perfect. I used a dictionary, went on Wikipedia, and coerced my friends and family to help. But at the end of

it all I ended up scrapping the entire thing and just going back to my own intuitive version; the one from above that had originally just sort of "flowed" out of me (about writing and humanity rising). And you know what? I really liked it. I still knew that I had to shorten it however, and I can't very well advise you to do something without doing it myself, so...

HERE'S MY END-RESULT:
I WRITE... THAT THEY MAY RISE.

For those of you that haven't done the previous exercises in the book, but kept reading this part anyway, you still have a chance to use this method, but you may want to go back and complete those areas first. Actually you can stop and do them now, if you like. If not, may I suggest you use one of the other methods listed below as you may find that they work better for you.

METHOD TWO – VARYING REPETITION

This method keeps very close to its title. When it says "varying repetition" it means it! In fact, if you find yourself stuck at all while using this method, simply go back to the title (varying repetition) and re-apply it to what you are writing. This will make sense when you do it. But I will explain it anyway, just in case.

Ask yourself why you became a SuperHero in the first place, and you will have just begun to write your mission statement with this method. Try to answer this question a few times, in a few different ways (Get it now? Varying repetition.). Anyway, write the answers down each time. This part is critical. You'll soon see that this method does require a lot of trial and error (and paper)... but it does work, and it is worth it.

Afterwards, take a look at your answers to that question. Next, take out the key phrases that you liked best from each one of those answers and recombine them in a way that summarizes all of the best parts. See what I mean about varying repetition? But believe me, it works. The real challenge with this method is not to get bored, or worse, to think you have done all you could and then give up.

Here's an example of the process:

QUESTION 1)
What is my single purpose in SuperHero life?

ANSWERS:
Now answer it in a few different ways and write down each answer.

QUESTION 2)
Now ask the same question in a different way, perhaps like so: **When I think about telling the world what I stand for, what's the dominant reason in my head?**

ANSWERS:
Now answer that one in a few different ways and write down each answer.

QUESTION 3)
Now ask your original question in a different way, perhaps like this: **Why did I answer the call—what reason jumped out at me?**

ANSWERS:
Now answer this new question in a few different ways and write down each answer.

Feel free to use things like: What moves me? What stirs the fire in my soul?, etc. Whatever it is that you think, will help to get you to the desired outcome. Of course these are only suggestions. Use them. Make your own. Most importantly, notice that they are all designed around the same question, they are just different ways to get there. This is the real trick to this method. Find the right question and this will solve itself.

When you are done with that step, the next step is pretty easy:

⇨ **1** Look at just your answers

⇨ **2** Takeout the key phrases that you liked best from each one of those answers

⇨ **3** Recombine them in a way that summarizes all of the best parts

⇨ **4** Now you're done. Turn that into your 1-2 sentence mission statement.

METHOD THREE – THE PATH

This next method comes from a book called The Path by Laurie Beth Jones. Here is a summary of what she suggests. Before you use this method though, you may want to pick up a copy of her book for the following reasons:

⇨ **1** She explains it better than I (and she should… it's her system).

⇨ **2** She offers you a complete background on her system and not just the abbreviated version shown here.

⇨ **3** She illustrates the success of others that have used her system.

⇨ **4** She offers you a complete list of verbs from which to choose (my friends found this to be extremely helpful).

⇨ **5** She helps you write a vision statement as well.

Basically her system boils down to a three-piece puzzle. In it she states,

> "[E]very mission requires action, and action words are verbs, so....
>
> puzzle piece 1 = choosing 3 verbs
>
> puzzle piece 2 = core values
>
> puzzle piece 3 = the group or cause which most moves/excites you."

To my way of thinking, the system identified in <u>The Path</u> really came down to simply completing the puzzle pieces and then crafting your masterpiece. The book is more than just these pieces however. I found two really powerful ideas in it that I would like to share here as well. Both of them are the words of the author. In it she says:

> "[Life began] to make a dramatic shift. Decision making came more easily, because now I had something against which to measure my activities. I learned firsthand the terror and majesty and power of having an exciting mission statement—one that says 'this is what I'm about.' I began to shed my fears about losing or not having a job, since I knew I would always have my mission, and any job I got would have to be an expression of that."

And also

> "Forgetting your mission leads, inevitably, to getting tangled up in the details."

METHOD FOUR – THE INTERNET

With a quick Google search I found these templates (http://www.timethoughts.com). You may also of course, write your own from scratch. The power of it lies in your commitment and how seriously you take this part of your journey, not in the templates themselves. Before you go on to them, you may also want to do a search on the Internet for yourself... who knows, your perfect model may be just around the corner.

> "To ... [what you want to achieve, do or become] ... so that ... [reasons why it is important]. I will do this by ... [specific behaviors or actions you can use to get there]."

> "To live each day with ... [choose one to three values or principles]... so that ... [what living by these values will give you]. I will do this by ... [specific behaviors you will use to live by these values]."

"To treasure above all else ... [most important things to you] by ... [what you can do to live your priorities]."

"To be known by ... [an important person/group]... as someone who is ... [qualities you want to have]...; by ... [some other person/group]... as someone who is ... [other qualities]."

It's probably obvious, so I won't spend much time on it. To use the templates above, all you must do is replace the part in [brackets] and fill in your own goals and ideas. It may feel a little like you are doing a mission statement Mad-Lib, but believe me, they work. Like the other methods, these are just guides. Feel free to change not just the part in brackets, but the other parts too, if you like. You are unique. Your mission statement should be as well.

THAT'S (ALMOST) **A WRAP**

Before you move on in your journey to become a SuperHero, it is essential you complete the task of writing your mission statement. It will act as an important guide for what comes next. Don't just think out some vague notion of your mission—write it down. This is not a task you can ignore if you wish to succeed. Indeed the SuperHeroes of the future will be those with the focus to achieve their goals and complete their mission.

MY MISSION:

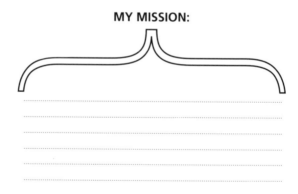

....
....
....
....
....
....

THE MISSION STATEMENT TEST:

Say your mission statement aloud. How does it feel? Does it suit you? Does it call you to action? Does it feel powerful? Is it a solid direction to your future? Does it give you an idea of what to do next (both at work and at home)?

Your mission statement, now that it is complete, is taking you somewhere. "Where?" you might ask. "Into the future," I reply. "And where, is that exactly?" you say. Well it's wherever you want it to be. And to help you create it, we next move to the vision statement. It's a simple matter, really.

WRITING YOUR VISION STATEMENT

Vision statements describe the future as you imagine it in five to ten years. They address the best of the best—the highest good you can achieve. What is your ideal future ten years from now? Think about it—really dream! And be flowery—it's ok to say things like "I live in a world that refuses to play victim. We are not the aggressors of ages past. By acting with the complete powers of my soul I have arrived at place of great vision. We are a united people of power, and we protect, we do not project. There are many that have taken up the gauntlet and helped to defeat those great robber-barons of malice and hatred. We are many. We are one."

Make it something that will motivate and inspire you! Here is a little instruction guide:

Close your eyes and imagine it's now ten years into the future. View the world, or perhaps even your SuperHero self as it will be then. Visualize things as if you were living them now.

Next, dream big… dream really big! In fact, dream bigger than big. Make your vision for the future include things you think may not even be really possible. Whatever your best possible outcome is, surpass it. It's okay… this is your dream.

WHAT DOES THE FUTURE LOOK LIKE?

WHAT DOES IT FEEL LIKE TO BE YOU?

CAN YOU HEAR ROARING CROWDS?

IN WHAT AREAS HAVE YOU ACHIEVED THE GREATEST SUCCESS?

This is your perfect world. Make it emotional. What do these things make you feel? Fully develop this imagery in your mind's eye. This is the dream. This is the visualization portion. When you can see it all clearly, and it really showcases your perfect future, then and only then are you ready to start writing it. When you are ready: open your eyes and write your vision statement. That's it. It's that simple.

When you do, however, there are a few rules to be applied here as well. Remember what we said above about using SuperHero language? Well this is definitely the place to use it. Also, remember to make it in the present tense. Do not say things like, "I will one day become whatever." If you say it like this you will never achieve it. Instead, say, "I am now the greatest whatever." Make it today.

What would the world look like if it no longer needed a SuperHero? What would you look like if you were the world's greatest SuperHero? Let it inspire you. The more specific, the more emotional, the stronger your statement is, the better! One final piece of instruction: construct a summarizing phrase that will bring back the imagery of your statement that you can look at quickly. If you need to, you can write this part last.

A FINAL WORD

Your vision is the future. Your mission gets you there. Your strategy is the way. Your tactics are the means. Changes in your strategy, mission or vision would be major decisions, and changes in your tactics and daily activities would be minor ones. We have yet to touch on all of these, but we will. Much, much more will be coming later. For now: write out your vision statement.

And get ready... the road ahead is about to get exciting!

> *"Whoever I am, or whatever I am doing, some kind of excellence is within my reach."—John W. Gardner (American Writer and Secretary of Health, Education and Welfare, 1912-2000)*

MY VISION

Let's liven things up a bit. That last chapter felt a little too much like work! In the next chapter we will plan some great adventures. (How about shark-diving?) Now of course you will still need to take the initiative and actually accomplish them, but believe me this next chapter will be the most exciting and fun chapter of the book... and the things you do there, will stay with you for a lifetime.

The Man, the Myth, the Legend

A FIRST LOOK AT WRITING YOUR OWN MYTHOLOGY

A First Look at Writing Your Own Mythology

How does your list look so far? Well, by now you know what makes a SuperHero; you know that you can become one; you know about friends, foes, and alliances; you have a mission statement (not a mission—those will come later, once you are a real SuperHero); and you have a vision statement. What could be left?

Next on our list is a mythology. You need one. In fact, you need it to sing your praises before you even have any praises to sing. I will tell you why in a minute. So… where does one get a good mythology you ask? Write one. Yes, I am suggesting that you write about your own exploits long before you even have them.

Why write your own mythology? Well, in the words of Jim Rohn, "If you don't design your own life plan, chances are you'll fall into someone else's plan. And guess what they have planned for you? Not much." Pretty much sums it up, don't you think? So, according to this, the first reason to write your own mythology is:

➡1. SO THAT YOU ACTUALLY HAVE A PLAN TO USE TO GO FORWARD.

Look at it like this, if you don't start moving towards a goal at some point, it will never get done. There's just no way that it can. So in a minute I will help you start a plan; not just some list of goals that you have always wanted to accomplish, but the stuff of legend. The real SuperHero mythology that will be sung, told, and retold, about you. After they are written, you go do them. It's simple, it's elegant, and it's complete. Most importantly though: it's a heck of a lot of fun. Just imagine a life filled with nothing but living out adventures and you'll have some idea of what I mean.

➡ 2. SO THAT YOU HAVE A LEGACY ON WHICH TO LOOK BACK.

Afterwards, once this is all finished (and not just the planning, but all of it: the designing, the writing, the accomplishing, the great life, etc.), once this is all done, you will now have a fantastic legacy. Certainly to some there may not seem to be any value in a legacy, and that's ok. In fact, let's not label this as wrong, or even uninformed. Let's call it… unexamined. For what is history if not the recorded version of someone's legacy?

Everyone knows that history is written by the winners. Why is this the case? Let's answer that question with another question. How possible is it for the losers to get their version out to the public? Well, with very few exceptions, it is all but impossible. This brings us to the next reason to write your own mythology.

➡ 3. SO THAT NO ONE ELSE CAN DO IT FOR YOU AND GET IT WRONG.

This is one of the bigger concepts (although it is sandwiched somewhere in the middle). Most people are stuck in their story, and we mentioned this in the last chapter. What does this mean? Well, to many people, the story of an event becomes more real than the actual event. How many times have you met a person who just had to tell you their story? There's a funny anecdote that Tad James (an expert in NLP or Neuro-Linguistic Programming) tells that explains this neatly. "If you tell most people to walk from here to the other side of the room, and they run into an obstacle, what do you think they do?"

When I first heard this, like most people I thought, "Oh, well they stop obviously." As Tad James and his wife Adriana point out, they don't stop. In fact what they do is much funnier, and so much more true: "They pick it up. They actually pick up the obstacle and carry it with them. And then, when they run into someone else, they show them what they're carrying. They say, 'Hey, look at this huge obstacle I'm carrying. Man I would have been so much farther along had I not had this obstacle to carry.'" It's silly, but it's true.

This is what's meant by being stuck in your story. Let it go, it's no longer relevant. No matter what you may think about that story from the past, it has no say about who you are today, and even less to say about the person you will be tomorrow. So don't keep referring to it, and don't let it keep holding you back.

Let's look at it another way. What is the difference between being a survivor, and being resilient? Many people will tell you that they have survived this thing or that; maybe rape, genocide, home-invasion, bankruptcy. Certainly you can see these all as terrible things. But when you say that you are a survivor of any particular event, then you must, by definition, carry that traumatic experience with you, in order to validate the story. After all, the story makes no sense unless it is tied to you in some way. But that is exactly what makes you stuck in it. You have to always be associated with it in order to say that you survived it. With this verbiage you will never be free. It also becomes a crutch that explains why you are not where you could have been, or perhaps as far along as should have been (as mentioned above).

Conversely, if you change your verbiage to saying that you are not a survivor, but that you are instead resilient, you drop the weight of any one particular story, and instead ascribe a strong characteristic to yourself. "Ah-ha," they will say. "Look at that person. They are so strong, so resilient." This is much more productive then always playing the victim to the tune of, "Oh... poor Joe. Did you know he was the survivor of a terrible _____." Yep. Poor Joe.

Changing your verbiage from survivor to resilient also has the advantage of drawing us out of the past and into the future (or at the very least, it brings us into our present). A characteristic like resilience proclaims how you handle things, while a memory will always be in the past. Stop living in the past.

So then let's apply this new learning to our bullet point. If you *are* going to have a story, at least make it one that you have consciously created and then have written for yourself. Make it one that you have judiciously phrased in the positive (and hopefully in the proactive). Be forward thinking about it. Avoid having it being written by someone else's thoughts of you, or worse, by your own lack of thoughts of yourself. Don't pretend that you have only been tossed about on the tumultuous waves in this great storm of life, and that you are but the chronicler. It is a great adventure... and I have to tell you, great adventures are cool. Really cool. This brings us to our next bullet point.

➡ 4. HAVING YOUR OWN MYTHOLOGY MAKES YOU LOOK COOL

Ok, sure, this one is meant somewhat in jest. But let's be honest. If we all have to be sitting here in this great big classroom anyway, we might as well get something out of it. Listen, I bet that for all of your dreams, from whenever they started, that they all have some sort of cool-factor about them. Even if it was just cool to you, and to no one else, the urge is still there. Something intangible that lies below the surface; something that makes you practically lust after the goal. And how many people do you know with their own mythology anyway? Talk about cool? You're like Beowulf!

➡ 5. IT WILL MAKE GREAT FODDER FOR THAT NOVEL YOU'VE ALWAYS SAID YOU'D WRITE.

Not only will the mythology itself make up a fantastic section for that book, the actual events and doings that come from being a SuperHero will also. Can you even imagine? You: a SuperHero. Oh the stories you'll tell. Remember the time you...? Or what about the time when you looked around and all you could see was...? It was almost like your own personal theme song was playing in the background. Or even cooler, playing in your headphones while you moved so effortlessly, so in the zone, so amazingly. How do you ever do it?

WHAT IS A MYTHOLOGY?

Ok, perhaps now you have a reason to actually want to write your own mythology, but what is it exactly? A mythology is a history, a bard's tale if you will. It's the magical telling of all your doings. It will be the praises they sing, the laments they tell, the adventurous tales by the fire with which they warm themselves in the winter months. It is a record, yes. But it can also be so much more. Rather than only telling them of what happened in the past, you are also setting up the accomplishments, goals, and amazing deeds of your own future. You are setting in motion the events that will shape the rest of your life.

By writing it yourself you become the architect, the creator and mastermind behind all your own adventures (and misadventures). Here's what's so great about writing it now, in advance: None of it has happened yet. So you can make the plans, set-up the dates, and literally fly off into the great unknown to experience it. You can really live it! You can actually make all of it happen. And now is the time to start.

READY, SET, MYTH

Wouldn't it be nice to have an easy way to start writing your own mythology? Wouldn't it be great to have it just handed to you? Guess what? Ka-Bam! Here it is! In fact, here are a few. Take your pick. We have:

* **The Tombstone Test**
* **An End to a Means**
* **The Hub McCann**
* **The Adventurer's List**
* **The Rock Star**

TOMBSTONE TEST AS A MYTHOLOGY

Here's a funny question: What would you have done in your life, if by the end of it, you had become someone amazing? Would you have stood up against a school bully? Would you have vigorously protested a war? Ran for public office? Sailed a boat around the world perhaps? What will they say about you when it is all over and done with?

In the movie Fight Club (1999. 20th Century Fox) this question was phrased a little differently:

TYLER
   What will you wish you'd done before you died?
RICKY
   Paint a self-portrait.
MECHANIC
   Build a house.
TYLER
   (to Jack)
   And you?
JACK
   I don't know! Nothing!
TYLER
   If you died right now, how would you feel about your life?

This is where the Tombstone test comes in. You simply decide what you want it to say on your tombstone, and then work backwards from there. You work backwards because, now that you have written it, it is your job—no, your very duty—to go accomplish it. In fact, let's start now. Is this creepy? What will it say after you die?

AN END TO A MEANS

If that way was too abrupt, or perhaps didn't work for you, here's another way. It starts with a question and then includes an easy exercise. The question is this "If you could see tomorrow, what would you do differently today?" The exercise that goes along with it is easier than the question, I think. It's certainly quicker, and possibly a lot more fun. In fact, the exercise is actually the key to answering the question. Without it, the question seems a lot more rhetorical than it really is. With it, the question basically answers itself. Now for the exercise.

> **❝If you don't design your own life plan, chances are you'll fall into someone else's plan. And guess what they have planned for you? Not much. JIM ROHN**

Go to MagMyPic.com and choose a magazine cover that means something to you. Here's how it worked for me. I went. I picked out Time Magazine, put my face on the cover and then decided what I wanted it to say in the caption. Man of the Year was too obvious and seemed like just a shortcut. So I really began to think about it.

Basically, it all went like this. My first thought was, "Which magazine should I pick?" Ok, based on the choices they had there was only one that was Time. Then which really served my need... and me would I choose for of course, the obligatory "Which picture of my trip to Paris, when I stood the world to see?" I found one that I liked from what caption? In other words, atop the Sacré-Coeur. And then of course, why was I there? What was it if I had made the cover of Time Magazine, Shop and added the caption that for, this great honor? So I went into Photo-Shop and added the caption that I thought said it best. It seemed to fit.

The first attempt was: The Man Who Changed Everything. It was good for starters but a little campy. I went back at it and after a few attempts ended up with: The Face of Consciousness. If you are interested in what that means you can read some of my other work—it's better covered there. Although if you are paying attention you may have already picked up a few bits and pieces. The point I am making here is that I thought out exactly what the cover would say. And not only what it would say *to me*, but what it would say to the world about me.

This was powerful because I then decided that I would have to now live up to that standard. You can't just say something like that and not create it. Would I be the person who changed everything? Perhaps. Am I conscious? Definitely. But it isn't like I simply chose something that was easy, or something that was true of me already. You see, true consciousness means limitless power. I liked that. It also means limitless compassion and understanding. I loved that. I now had a goal. I had a journey. And it also gave me the start of both my mission and my mythology.

In order to do this, in order to write your own mythology, you have to start seeing the ending as a beginning. Why? Because it gives you structure. It gives you goals. And it lets you consciously design where you are going to end up. Whatever you determine to be your legacy, your global goal perhaps, you have to clearly define, and then advance towards it. You have to start now.

THE HUB MCCANN

Did that mythology method not work either? Maybe you're just weighing your options... Or maybe you liked it, but perhaps you wanted to add something more? Here's an option for doing just that. Best of all, it leverages your past experiences to help you get a jump-start.

Some of you, though you may not yet be a SuperHero, have already amassed more than a few exciting stories. This is the perfect starting point in writing your mythology. For example, in my own life there was that time in India I battled against an entire roomful of badge-wielding thugs. Or the time I fell six stories and walked away from it without a scratch. Or twice walking unharmed through gunfire... Stopping a would-be rapist in the act... Scaling the side of a hotel in Los Angeles without any equipment... helping orphans in Malaysia... or being trapped in a notorious crack alley in South Central... you get the idea. (All true, by the way.)

So why is this called the Hub McCann? Because one of the characters in the movie Second-hand Lions (2003. New Line Cinema), when accosted by a bully, was asked "Hey, who do you think you are, huh?" His amazing reply inspired me that day. It was:

"I'm Hub McCann. I've fought in two world wars, and count-less smaller ones on three continents. I've led thousands of men into battle with everything from horses and swords to artillery and tanks. I've seen the headwaters of the Nile and tribes of natives

*no white men had ever seen before. I've won and lost a dozen for-
tunes, killed many men, and loved only one woman with a passion a
flea like you could never begin to understand. That's who I am."*

That's Hub McCann… and that's one hell of a mythology.

THE ADVENTURER'S LIST

Here's another way to write your own mythology. It is called: The Adventurer's List. Sometimes I like to call it: The Reverse Hub McCann. But no matter what you call it, it works.
And it works really simply.

First you create an Adventurer's List… then you go do it. It's really straight-forward. For example, remember that time you went shark-diving in and among those huge Great Whites
(SharkDiver.com)… Or perhaps the time you hand-carried medical supplies to those children in Mexico (VolunteerMatch.com, Rotary.org)… What about when you took to the
streets to fight crime in your neighborhood (MadDads.com, GuardianAngels.org). Yes, you
literally make a list of all the things you want to do and then you go do them, but it isn't
about thrill-seeking. Because it's a mythology, you choose things that are related to who
you are as a SuperHero. You relate them to your goals, and you relate them to your mission
statement. It's a process… but it works.

One of the major differences between the SuperHero and the average Joe (no offense, Joe),
is the defined mission. The SuperHero knows his goal because he wrote it for himself. He
clearly understands his mission. He pursues them both relentlessly. It is this self-applied
definition that makes him different from you; it is this self-applied definition that makes
him better.

THE ROCK STAR

This technique is aimed specifically at the Freelancer. With the Freelancer comes a certain
dedication to duty shared by all SuperHeroes, but the Freelancer has made their career the
object of their focus. The risk is that, with of all their focus and attention spent on their
daily jobs or improving their skill-set, they may have just forgotten how to dream. And you
can't write a mythology if you can't dream. So let's change that.

Think of your dream job. Not a good job, your dream job. Perhaps you are working at a
great company right now, but want to change positions there, or maybe take your skills
and form a new company that does something similar. Maybe you would like to completely change your career. Whatever it is, imagine yourself doing that job right now.

Do you have it? Now fast-forward that scene in your mind until you are the highest, best,
and most famous person to have ever held that job. Do you like that lifestyle? What is it

you like about it? What do you find to be the most fun and exciting part? Better still for our purposes: Where do you see the most adventure? These are the things on which you base your mythology.

Start writing from this point. Write about all your greatest exploits as you traveled the globe in search of an undiscovered species, or perhaps you were a great firefighter who single-handedly rescued scores of people, whatever it is, start your mythology here, and then start your SuperHero life here as well.

By the way, if after doing the exercise, you find that you don't like playing that role (the highest, best, most famous to have ever done that job), then you may not want to take the job. If you do take it, and ignore this warning, then you'll always be conflicted and sabotage yourself to keep from advancing and ever reaching that spot. If on the other hand you love it, then yes, by all means, have at it.

IDEA STARTERS FOR MY MYTHOLOGY
(Circle One):

My Dream Job | My Adventurer's List | My Accomplishments

....
....
....

FINAL TIPS

Take this section seriously. These exercises, just like the ones before, are not things you can do in your head. They must be written down, and done so in great detail. It is your clarity of vision that will guide you. Think things through, decide… and then write. If it helps you can free write for a few minutes. Write down everything! Write the most fantastic things you can think of wanting for yourself! Be serious but also be honest about what you want for yourself. Throw away your limited concept of realism. Understand that anything, literally anything, can be real.

If you really want to have fun with it, you could even devise characters and challenges to overcome. See how easy it is? Get creative! Have fun with it! You are writing more than just a mythology right now. You are writing the rest of your life. A SuperHero is trained in many aspects and can call on many different skills, creative writing is just one more. Let's call it: being in control of your life.

Once you have visualized surmounting all of the obstacles on your list, wrap up the story. Not sure how to end it? Look closer. You already have your tombstone test as the ending. Just try to create a picture of how you want your life to look as a whole.

Consider how much more powerful it is to design your life than it is to wake up one morning toward the end of it all and wonder how you got there with nothing to show for it and no great dreams ever having been accomplished. By writing about it, you are taking conscious control of every aspect and every decision. You will think about how every choice will affect your goals for yourself. Can you imagine a more ideal Super-Power than creating literally everything that you want in your life? The person with the clearest conception of the outcome will always be the one to prevail, and this is also a valid lesson for battle.

Your mythology doesn't have to be grammatically correct. It doesn't have to have structure, dramatic tension or be a perfect literary achievement. These are simply your future plans. You don't have to ever even show it to anyone else. You can keep it locked in a drawer if you would like. But do keep it. Read it periodically, and remember to always check things off your list as you do them. It will help motivate you and keep you motivated as you go through your training.

One of the best parts of this exercise is that unlike a tombstone, your mythology is not written in stone. You are simply committing to paper what is important to you, what you want to achieve right now. You are only truly accountable to yourself. This being said, if your mission changes, if you become interested in new things, or your life takes you in a new direction, don't be afraid to do the exercise over again.

For those of you who are still deciding certain aspects of your SuperHero life, this will still be a powerful exercise. It will help you consider what is important to you now. Perhaps, you simply have never done that before today. The point here is to keep you focused on the goals YOU want for YOURSELF. These exercises, and the SuperHero training you will later endure, should never feel like a chore. They are only for the purpose of achieving everything you desire. Never settle, never give up. You can do everything and anything!

LIVING THE DREAM

You've probably noticed that all of these methods have something in common. The reason for this is because no matter which one you pick to help you to write your mythology, you still have to take the next step and live it out.

> *"Whatever you can do, or dream you can, begin it. Boldness has genius, power and magic in it."*
> —Goethe.

Yes, your adventure does begin with the writing. But it will never materialize until you act on it. They say that life is what happens while you are making great plans for it. This trap is easy to fall into, but it is nearly always fatal for the SuperHero. You must act. You must move forward. Or you will perish.

Either way, you will become what you choose to become. It will either be based on your solid planning and execution, or it will be based on your inability to follow-through. It is always this way because we write our own roles. We are not victims. More accurately, you are what you say you are.

To prove this point, I offer you one simple challenge: Simply notice that when you meet someone new they tend to put you into a category; a sort of mental box, if you will. Watch what happens when you start adding things to your personal description that are out of the norm. "Hi, I'm a smoke-jumper. Nice to meet you." All of a sudden, people don't place you in the average category anymore. Give it a shot. Make yourself a little sound-bite (perhaps something as powerful as the words of Hub McCann, if you're up to it). You will be glad you did. A word of advice however: when you do this, use something legitimate. There's no sense in making something up—I mean even Indiana Jones is still a part-time professor. Use this as a chance try out not only your new mythology, but also your new life as a SuperHero.

> *"The bravest are surely those that have the clearest vision of what lies before them, danger and glory alike and yet notwithstanding go out to meet it. For whole Earth is a sepulcher of famous men and their story is not only graven in stone over their native land, but, lives on far away without visible symbol, woven into the stuff of other men's lives."*
>
> *—Thucydides*

Team Players

A FIRST LOOK AT LONERS, SIDEKICKS, DUOS AND LEAGUES

A First Look at Loners, Sidekicks, Duos and Leagues

As you continue onward in this journey of becoming a SuperHero, the road ahead is fraught with a dark ambiguity. You have chosen your life's mission and know where it is that you now must head. You have shown us your grand vision. You shall now choose who you will take by your side, if anyone. Remember: the only standard is the one that you set for yourself. Now then, read each section and decide carefully exactly which path your journey will take.

THE RATIONALE

There is a reason that this section has followed all the others (and didn't come any sooner). In the choice of whether or not to take a partner, to join a team, or to walk the road alone, you must first be a complete individual in your own right. The true SuperHero is already complete. Furthermore, in our case, it is not just being a complete individual that is important, you must also be a complete SuperHero before you can partner up.

The only exception to this rule is the rise to power. If you are training with someone, and you both are on the journey, then partnerships are encouraged. Highly encouraged, in fact.

The need to be complete in your own right is why you were originally tasked to decide many of the small things first. Things like who you were, and whether you were going to be bad or good (to use the conventional, mere mortal terms), were critical at this level because the answers to these questions had to come from you and not from associations with others.

This is also why you had to choose for what you would stand and where you wanted to head. You had to know your goals, your direction, your obstacles, and even your best possible outcome. And now you do. Therefore, only now can you truly decide if you will join forces with another. I caution you, however, to not take on a partner or even a team unless they are as committed as you. Otherwise, it will end in disaster. Your best insurance, therefore, is to make sure your potential partners have gone through these steps as well.

In this chapter you will find a few warm-up questions to get you thinking about the topic of SuperHero partnerships. You may even find it valuable to consider your past. For example: How well did you work on group projects when you were in school? Examining the lessons of your youth is always valuable, and it will give you a more complete picture of yourself, which is critical in determining who you wish to be.

You may of course choose to not use the lessons of your past, and instead choose to become someone completely different going forward than the person you were; perhaps choosing even to be someone different from the person you are today. One piece of advice however: if you do decide to completely change who you are, you cannot simply run from what is already inside of you. You must first recognize and accept all that you are now, before you can move on from it. Don't worry though: the most exciting part of this is that it is all up to you! You hold the keys to your design, right here in your hands, right now.

HELPFUL HINTS

In understanding the following examples, look at how well your SuperHero goals and your current lifestyle choices complement each other. It makes your life much easier if you don't have to up-end everything to get the results you seek.

Also, while looking at these examples remember: it is your choice. For now the goal is simply to get you thinking about your SuperHero self in complete detail. All choices, both major and minor, are yours to make. How you decide to meld, or not meld, the different categories are up to you. Just make sure to begin your SuperHero training with the strongest understanding of these basic concepts as possible.

Don't worry if this seems overwhelming right now. You own the book. It's not going anywhere. Also, you're in control of your own destiny. For my part, I'm not merely here to just show you a door and hope you walk in. I am here to show you a long corridor of doors. You may choose the one you like.

A FINAL WORD, BEFORE WE JUMP IN:

This chapter can actually be skipped by some of you, as your progress has been tremendous. It is in fact probably the only chapter that can be skipped for that matter. The others are too important.

So, if you already know the answer to whether or not you will be partnering up... then skip it. I left it in the book for those that needed help finding the answer.

SuperHeroes are action-takers. If you are ready, complete the exercises for this chapter, and then move on to reading the next one instead.

I will see you over there soon.

LONERS

There are many SuperHeroes that were loners and they succeeded quite well, without even taking on a sidekick. Consider Spider-Man, Captain America, Superman, Wonder Woman, or the Silver Surfer, for example. There is also Jason Bourne, and James Bond, of the cinema world, or Sidney Bristow from the TV show Alias. Even Batman, before he met Robin was an accomplished, lone vigilante.

If you idolize one of these SuperHeroes, or perhaps aspire to be like one of them, you may decide that being the lone SuperHero is the path you wish to take. Indeed you will find few disadvantages should you choose to do so. If you have taken seriously the point of chapter two (in that what you write, you create), and that we are each powerful beings, then you will understand that, even alone you can complete your mission.

In making the Loner/Partner decision, you may find it valuable to consider:

* **Whether or not you are self-motivated**
* **If you respond better to goals when motivated by another**
* **Whether or not you actually enjoy working on your own**
* **Whether or not you often enjoy taking your leisure time alone as well**

Some people, of course, thrive on being alone, on spending time by themselves. It allows them to better focus and clears up their thinking process. Keep in mind though, once your SuperHero training begins, you will be required to focus that much more often. If you have chosen to train by yourself, this will involve you being alone even more than you may currently be, which brings with it its own challenges and risks. Like all things, being a loner has both positive and negative things associated with it.

There are comic book heroes and also well-known, real people, across history that have accomplished great things by acting alone, motivated completely by themselves. Often, it is only by acting against conventional wisdom that real change takes place.

There are also certain professions that lend themselves to isolation. Depending on your hero type, you may fall into this category and find huge benefits by tuning out the distractions. Take writers, for example. I ask you, would Emily Dickinson or JD Salinger (both loners), have been half as successful with a familial brood snapping at their heels? Dickinson spent the last sixteen years in her house living alone, and most of her work was found after her death.

Salinger was even more extreme in his reclusive behavior. After his success with <u>Catcher in the Rye</u>, he turned down interviews and refused requests that his picture appear on jacket covers. Salinger shut himself inside his New Hampshire home, where he remains to this day. These specific authors are great examples because they are known as being among the most talented writers of their time. And their lifestyle choice did not at all interfere with their goals. But just because it worked for them, will it also work for you?

In sports, Joe DiMaggio and Barry Bonds were labeled as loners. In their world, however, things turned out differently. The fact that both were loners led to their being negatively perceived by the press. Sportswriters regularly criticized DiMaggio for his habits of keeping to himself and also of his arranging a small, private funeral for his ex-wife, Marilyn Monroe. Bonds has similar habits today: He trains on his own and does not interact very much with his teammates. Consequently, it is only too easy to find negative press about him.

Of course as a SuperHero (and depending on your goals) negative publicity may be exactly the thing you don't want.

On the other hand, people are also sometimes suspicious of loners, because it is so hard to get to know them. But maybe this is exactly what you want for your SuperHero self to gain an air of mystery. Many SuperHeroes (such as Batman), maintained this effect of mystery quite well, and often used it to great advantage in battling their enemies.

If you do choose the path of the lone SuperHero, it may also be valuable to consider what resources you'll have at your disposal to help you accomplish your tasks. For example, even Batman had his butler Alfred who helped him run both the house and the Batcave. Just because you are a loner, doesn't mean you have to be alone. You can do your SuperHero work alone, and still have people in your life that motivate, help, and push you.

Finally, though some loners meet with a self-destructive end, the two items don't always correlate. Choosing to be a loner will not make you the next Emily Dickinson, nor will it cause you to shoot your classmates. It is up to you to choose what the effect of being a loner will be.

SIDEKICKS

Before I move on to duos and groups, I would like to take a minute to discuss sidekicks. While sidekicks have their place in SuperHero history, I am specifically recommending against them. The problem with having a sidekick is that it undermines the idea that anyone can be a SuperHero, and truthfully: anyone can be. A person who chooses to be a sidekick is putting limitations on themselves, and basically slighting everything of which they are truly capable.

This does not mean you shouldn't have a SuperHero partner to go along with you—please see the section on Duos below. The difference is that the role of each person in a duo is equal, while the role of a sidekick is not.

Also... the role of sidekick is not like some entry-level position that helps you get your foot in the door on the road to becoming a SuperHero. They usually go nowhere. Maybe it's a lack of confidence or self-drive, but being a sidekick is dead end. Sometimes literally.

Take Robin, the Boy Wonder, for example: His stories show only too well that being a sidekick does not always build a strong SuperHero foundation. While Batman and Robin were known as the Dynamic Duo, they weren't partners with equal roles. Batman was really more like a mentor to Robin. And even though Robin was one of the most successful sidekicks, his stories didn't always pan out.

I say "stories" because, as a matter of fact, there were actually at least five Robins in the DC comic series (talk about replaceable). The summary goes like this:

* Dick Grayson became Robin and succeeded to become a SuperHero called Nightwing.

* Jason Todd then became Robin and was literally voted to death by the reading public who called in on a 1-900 number to watch him die.

* Timothy Drake became Robin and did ok (he got his own comic book).

* Stephanie Brown became Robin but was then fired by Batman for not following directions, and was later killed.

* Another girl named Carrie Kelly then became Robin but she wasn't really part of a regular comic series so she sort of just... disappeared.

If that doesn't make a statement about the rather flimsy nature of sidekicks I don't know what does and, as I say, Robin was probably the most famous of them all.

One thing it does say, however, is that they were better received when it looked like they were on their way to becoming something valuable in their own right. Not when they were just tagging along. Really then, they were more like SuperHeroes in training. They weren't really full-fledged SuperHeroes yet, but they were on their way.

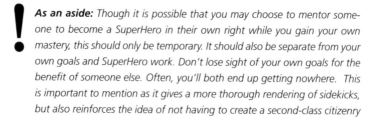

As an aside: *Though it is possible that you may choose to mentor someone to become a SuperHero in their own right while you gain your own mastery, this should only be temporary. It should also be separate from your own goals and SuperHero work. Don't lose sight of your own goals for the benefit of someone else. Often, you'll both end up getting nowhere. This is important to mention as it gives a more thorough rendering of sidekicks, but also reinforces the idea of not having to create a second-class citizenry in order to have better mission support.*

It is worth mentioning here that Stan Lee was also not a fan of sidekicks. The Marvel character Spider-Man, was a fifteen year old kid (Peter Parker) who gets bitten by a radioactive spider and is imbued with super-powers. By creating a SuperHero out of a teenager, Lee was sending the message that anyone could be a SuperHero and not just a sidekick. If a kid can handle not only the various nemeses terrorizing New York, but also the realistic problems of a teenager, then maybe we can all handle it as well. Let us heed his advice.

DUOS AND TEAMS

Great partnerships are everywhere. In the world of SuperHeroes, there are of course larger partnerships (Fantastic Four, X-Men, Avengers, Teen Titans) and smaller ones as well (the Wonder-Twins, Fro-Zone & Mr. Incredible, Power Man & Iron Fist, Green Lantern & Green Arrow) that often go out on missions together. We will cover the larger teams more in the next section. For now, let's consider the option of bringing on a partner.

PARTNERSHIP ETCETERAS

If you do choose to have someone help you in your quest, you must realize that they will almost always be around (even while you are at your most vulnerable). This being the case, you should choose a person that will freely choose to be by your side. And though this goes without saying, you want someone that you can trust completely for this important position. Who do you know right now that you would trust, that has similar values and goals to you that would be interested in becoming your SuperHero partner?

Now certainly this doesn't have to be a spouse or even a girlfriend or boyfriend. But it is important that there be complete trust and support in such an arrangement. Think about the vow you might take during a marriage ceremony. You are announcing your partnership to the world. This will happen with your SuperHero life as well.

In a marriage vow, you also take a vow to each other, to completely support the other person, no matter the circumstances (in sickness and in health, etc.). Can you see the value of such a vow in a SuperHero partnership? Now, I'm not suggesting SuperHero partners get hitched, but at least making a contract with your partner, especially if you may be involved in some perilous crime-fighting action, is a good idea to consider.

If you don't currently know anyone who fits that role, but you're still interested in having a partner, don't worry! In fact this is an even better scenario. As I have mentioned before, you need the person to be committed to it for their own reasons and not just because you two happen to be dating.

But I do still encourage you to at least *think* about friends that may evolve into playing the role of your SuperHero partner. There are so many examples of friends that went on to build amazing businesses and accomplish incredible tasks, that it would be a shame not to ponder the idea. Louis and Clark, in 1803 mapped out the western United States;

Ben and Jerry were friends in school and went on to build the famous ice cream business; or what about Stan Lee and Jack Kirby who came up with some of the most famous SuperHero comic stories of our time?

Having the right type of person as a partner, or even just present in your life, can bring out the best in you. Far too often, people seem to connect on shared dislikes. We can do so much more—anything we want, in fact—if we put our energy into the positive. This brings up peer pressure. Though it's often considered a negative thing, it can also be completely positive.

> **❝ People influence us all the time. Having the right influences are what make the difference.**

People influence us all the time. Having the right influences are what make the difference. If you always have people around you that are doing great things with their lives, then you are apt to do the same. This makes the people with whom you surround yourself, or with whom you spend time, a very important decision. This is a lesson that should be learned by all. The people in your life affect you. Make sure that it is positive. If your friends sit on the couch and watch TV all day, then this might become an excuse for you to do the same. Live among potential SuperHeroes and see just what you can create!

NAVY SEALS

Great things come out of being around powerful people, including outstanding teamwork. The US Navy SEAL (Sea, Air and Land) teams exude the importance of teamwork in their training and execution of missions. Everything is done as a team, with the remarkable result that no SEAL has ever been left behind in a mission. Part of the thought process behind their training is that if everyone is trained on a very high level, using teamwork, it is possible to complete missions that one man could not do alone. It also helps to have such a dependable support system in place.

There is a complete trust in your fellow team members when you know of what they are capable. The Navy SEALs are the best because they demand the best. Men from the United States Navy enter SEAL training voluntarily. Yet the physical demands are so harsh that training classes often lose 70-80% of their volunteers. That is a staggering fail rate. However, this system ensures the Navy SEALs are made up of only the most elite, ensuring their mission's success.

The example of the Navy SEALs demonstrates that we should demand the best of our part ers and of ourselves in order to achieve optimum results. Not everyone makes it through the training, as we have discussed. Does this mean that they can't? Or that they chose not to? Creating a team of elite members often has negative connotations because it seems exclusionary. However, let us strip away these connotations for a moment. Consider your own goals and what you are trying to achieve. Are you not reaching for the utmost you can achieve? And doesn't this involve demanding the very best? You know that it does. Be comfortable with creating standards and sticking to them. Be comfortable with establishing an elite standard. People who don't meet your standards are choosing to not meet them, they are settling by being comfortable with their own limitations.

What we can also take from the Navy SEALs is that it may be a good idea to go through SuperHero boot camp in Part II with your chosen partner. Even if you meet your partner while you are completing your training, make sure that when you two team up, that you push each other as much as possible. This will allow you two to know each other's strengths, and to help each other to become the strongest and most powerful SuperHero you can each be.

The example of having a spotter at the gym to help you lift weights is also a relevant example of why this is a good idea. Your spotter is there not only to protect you from hurting yourself (if a weight slips or if you cannot lift the weight any longer) but also to push you to your limits. This same result can be applied to your quest to becoming a SuperHero. Imagine if your goal was not to be able to bench press three hundred pounds, but instead to _____. (Yes, this is meant to be blank. Go ahead, fill it in! It will be empowering to see it in writing!)

If this was your goal, what could your spotter, or your SuperHero partner, help you accomplish? Maybe a better question is, what couldn't they help you accomplish? We see physical ability get pushed to extreme limits all of the time (body builders, stunt men, professional athletes, etc.). Why not bring this concept to everything we do? Why not push every limit we know? Why not become a SuperHero?

BIGGER TEAMS

If you are interested in becoming part of a SuperHero team, first look to your family. Families vary greatly by definition and size across cultures. No matter who your family is for you, usually this word means a group of people in your life that you completely trust, and that support you. Consider recruiting these people for the creation of a SuperHero team. A close-knit family may already share a set of ideals that would make a strong foundation for a SuperHero team.

It is also important to understand the difference at this point between founding a team and finding a team. Since founding a team means starting one, it will most likely be based on your own goals and ideals. The people joining you are probably joining the team because they understand and agree with ideals. Obviously then, founding a group will work best when there is already a group of people in your life that share a similar outlook. Consider the example of a close-knit family, as described above, or also the founding of Parkour by David Belle and his friends.

He was already friends with like-minded people who all valued physical capability. The group went on to start the Yamakasi, also made up of Yann Hnautra, Frédéric Hnautra, David Malgogne, Kazuma, and Sebastian Foucan. Afterwards Sebastian ventured off and founded the sport of Free Running (an idea we used to label one of our SuperHero types). As individuals they were talented; as a team they were legendary.

Finding a team, however, is slightly different. This refers to going out and finding people who share your interests, goals, and ideals. This doesn't mean that you all have to believe in exactly the same thing or even want the same things. It's not a cult after all. When you add to this the fact that your group will be a collaboration of people who all have different skills and goals, it will be important for you to not only have your own personal mission and vision statement, but also a group mission statement as well. It will keep you on track.

As pointed out in the very beginning of this chapter, it is important to retain your own sense of self (and of SuperHero-ness), even in a group. A group is not simply the melding of many people into one. It is strong because it combines all the differences of everyone, and moves them all in the same direction.

20,000 LEAGUES

If you are not sure where to start looking to find a team, have no fear. There are already a tremendous amount of people in the world that share your commitment to being a Super-Hero. Some are even sitting on a couch somewhere, reading this book. The Internet will be a valuable resource for you. Almost all current Real Life SuperHeroes (RLSHs) have web pages, MySpace pages or something of the sort. Search for some in your area (but don't be creepy!).

Also, citizenheroes.com (the website of Citizen Prime) recruits new people to rise and become SuperHeroes. There is a roster on his site of people who have already answered his call and who may be interested in finding a team to help them in their own quest.

If you are interested in finding others who have taken the SuperHero road described in this book however, then the place for you is definitely on our website, TheSuperHeroMovement.com. It has SuperHero resources, networking, contact information, and much more. The main benefit however is that it parallels this book and also your training. It will offer you things that you will find nowhere else. And that is a promise.

Well then, did you make a decision? Will your future SuperHero self have a partner? Or perhaps team members like the Fantastic Four? Or are you to become a lone vigilante, like the Batman? Commit to your decision! Write it down (making any notes you would like) and then keep reading!

TO PARTNER, OR NOT TO PARTNER...

HERE IS MY ANSWER:

○ LONER

○ DUO

○ SIDEKICK

○ TEAM / LEAGUE   ○ FIND A TEAM / BUILD A TEAM

○ OTHER:

. . . .

Potential Partners / Teams / Team Members Include:

Remember this is only the starting point. To truly become a SuperHero, you must continue to follow-through. You must move on to Part II and complete SuperHero Boot Camp (coming up quite soon). You must also complete Part III where you get to choose your superpowers. Your quest is now taking shape, your SuperHero identity is beginning to form. Do you feel it? Do you feel the energy rising within you? It is giving you the momentum you need to move forward, to propel you, so that you may also, someday soon, ascend.

You & Improved

A FIRST LOOK AT THE QUESTION OF IDENTITY

A First Look at the Question of Identity

So you've made it. That's quite a distance, really. Think I'm kidding? At this moment there are 6,859,480,895 people in the world. Look around. How many of them are Super-Heroes? When I tell you that you have come far… I mean it. If you have taken all of the required steps, and written things down, and not just thought about them, then you are ready for the next step in your journey: Creating your SuperHero Identity.

ISSUES OF IDENTITY CONSTRUCTION

There are many topics to consider in this chapter, so, to keep things organized, here is an overview of what is to come, including the subsection list.

➡ **SECRECY (with costumes, friends, marketing & publicity)**
- Covert or Overt
- Clothes Make the Man
- Tell Me Who Your Friends Are and I'll Tell You Who You Are
- The Market as Master

➡ **BRINGING TOGETHER THE IDENTIFYING ELEMENTS YOU'VE CREATED**
- Some Assembly Required

➡ **ADDING IN NEW PIECES LIKE A LOGO OR EMBLEM, A NAME, AND A SLOGAN**
- Read the Label
- What's in a Name

➡ **DESIGNING YOUR LOOK (absolutely a fun project)**
- Oh the Colors

➡ SECRECY

We begin by discussing whether or not you want the world to know who you are. Will your secret identity actually be secret? There are benefits and drawbacks here (as in most things), so let's take a look.

A SuperHero's path is so starkly different from those around them (considering how many people are trapped in their limitations) that as a result, many SuperHeroes choose to maintain a secret identity (and also lead a rather solo career path). One reason is so that they might be able to hold on to some semblance of a "normal life." Sometimes, of course, they also choose it to protect their families from retribution. Either way, so begins their double life.

A couple of the obvious double-life holders are Superman, whose alter ego was Clark Kent (a mild-mannered reporter), and Spider-Man whose alter ego was Peter Parker, (a photographer). These two at least, had day-jobs, and day-lives. It was better for them to live, to work, and to "SuperHero" alone, keeping people at a distance. This way no one ever made the connection between the two facets of their identities.

However in your case (to bring the concept closer to home), the idea of a double life may not be workable, or even desirable. First of all there certainly is some sacrifice to keeping the charade going, and honestly, once you tap in to all your glorious powers you may decide that you want to be a SuperHero all the time!

In other words it is quite possible that you will decide to bring your new, incredible abilities to every single thing you do, and taking a break from all your super-powers just to fool your friends and family might not hold very much interest for you.

• COVERT OR OVERT

In the comics, there are SuperHeroes on both sides of the fence—some public about their identities, others private. As mentioned above, in their world, there were sometimes serious concerns like protecting their loved ones from retribution. This, obviously, would lead some of them to create a double life. But there were also other reasons.

Sometimes the SuperHero image was designed to strike fear into criminals, and anonymity was just a bonus. And still other times there was the attempt at avoiding the stigma of being different. As you will come to see when you have to make some of these same decisions for yourself, each one comes down to something personal. These are all things the SuperHero takes into account when deciding how their life should be.

Some SuperHeroes chose to live publicly; that is to say they chose to live their lives as SuperHeroes under the public spotlight. Each had their own, specific reasons for doing this as well. Physically, some actually were their SuperHero selves and could not change (Thing, Silver Surfer). Others simply liked the attention.

As a side-note: It's a little misleading to say that all SuperHeroes without a secret identity are in fact public. For example, Wolverine hates everybody and just prefers to be left alone. This doesn't make him public as much as it just makes him not have a secret identity.

PUBLIC	PRIVATE
Iron Man	Batman
The Fantastic Four	Superman
The Silver Surfer	Spider-Man
Wolverine	Captain America

Non-Exhaustive, Happy-time List

• CLOTHES MAKE THE MAN

In the real world of course, things are slightly different. I say slightly because some of your reasons for going public (or not going public) might clearly match up with their reasons, while others might remain more personal. For example, you might not really be into the idea of a costume. You might think of it as silly. Maybe the stigma would keep you from taking yourself seriously.

On a personal note, I didn't find this to be the case. (I don't wear a costume... but I do understand them. Think of a police officer, or a fire-fighter if it helps.) To my mind, the costume is freeing. Also, the costume itself can become validating support for higher authority. Further, for all the times that I have been in uniform, I found that it readied me for what I was about to do. It set my mind to work, and changed me, even if only slightly. A costume (or uniform) allowed me to do what I could not have done in other clothes.

In this regard I am like the character Don Diego Vega who said:

> *"It is a peculiar thing to explain, señores. The moment I donned cloak and mask, the Don Diego part of me fell away. My body straightened, new blood seemed to course through my veins, my voice grew strong and firm, fire came to me! And the moment I removed cloak and mask I was the languid Don Diego again. Is it not a peculiar thing?" (Johnston McCulley, The Mark of Zorro).*

Another advantage provided by the costume is the opportunity to carry gadgets that would be otherwise unwieldy. It is a specially prepared garment, much like a police officer's uniform. The Sam Browne belt that cops often wear has many clips and rings that are extremely useful to an officer. Try carrying all of those gadgets in your sweat pants—I dare you.

Anonymity is of course a benefit as well. It can keep you from getting into hot water considering that everyone (and their brother) has a camera on them these days. Also, one assumption (perhaps incorrect) is that you will be in and around your own neighborhood.

Without a mask you might easily be targeted for retribution as well.

Before you move into the costume idea too readily though, I would advise you to first con- sider the drawbacks carefully. A costume means prep time, every time. What do I mean by this? I mean that if you don't have your gear you may find yourself unable to perform the task at hand. If trouble happens unexpectedly and you don't have your gear, you have a problem. On the other hand, if you are dressed in costume, just how would you get into a night-club dressed like that, anyway? See? It's a problem. Luckily for you I show you how to overcome this in Part III (with things like gadgetry).

Another issue with the costume is the perceived threat with law enforcement. A normal guy who helps out is one thing, an armed vigilante is quite another. Let's say you witness a crime and step in to help. In civilian clothes you have plausible deniability. In a costume you were seeking out confrontation.

And then of course there is the mask. Other than the obvious problem of freaking out the cops, if your mask is not made properly you will lose your peripheral vision. If you are the crime-fighting type of SuperHero, this is a deadly mistake. Also, it adds to the heat factor considering how much of our body heat escapes through our head. Sweating dehydrates you.

The last examples were of course focused mostly on the crime-fighting SuperHero type. But there are other types who might want to choose items in this area carefully as well. Say for example you are a Freelancer who specializes in "high-risk animal rescues." Again, you need a way to carry your gear in order to do your job. Weigh out the pros and cons before you commit.

• TELL ME WHO YOUR FRIENDS ARE, AND I'LL TELL YOU WHO YOU ARE

What about your friends and family? If you keep your activities a secret you may miss the opportunity for helpful insight. Let's look at the Freelancer type again. Let's say you are a lawyer and you have a high-profile project to work on for a big client. Perhaps you are re-structuring the corporate shield for them to enable them to move their assets off-shore. Wouldn't you want to be able to fully assemble your team and move in quickly and silently, prepared for battle? Well, if no one ever knows that you are an elite operative you might miss out on a lot of opportunities for advice, growth, and insight.

By the way, I just love the concept of a lawyer, doctor, officer, computer technician, what- have-you, moving in quickly and silently like an elite operative. Every line of work, every skill, has the opportunity to be performed flawlessly. Commitment, obsessive focus, qual- ity, and detail: these are the watchwords of the SuperHero.

One reason, perhaps the main reason in fact, that people who are undertaking the task of becoming a SuperHero don't tell others however, is the fear of failure. If it doesn't work, they don't want to look foolish. They don't want to be laughed at for trying to achieve more. If this is the case, don't worry. It's absolutely normal. But you need not always look at yourself to fix this. Instead, you might try looking at your peer group.

One reason you run the risk of chiding or teasing from them is because they like you. It may sound contradictory, but it's true. Either they fear your failure, or they fear your success. If you fail, they may feel bad for you. If you succeed, they may feel bad for themselves.

Look at it this way: If you change, and your peers don't, they will try to bring you back down again because A) They like hanging out with you, and they don't want you to change and leave, or B) If you are able to do it, and they haven't been able to do it, what does that say about them?

There is a little bit of selfishness in this, it's true, but it can be worked around. You also have the option of either bringing them up with you (which is really challenging unless it stems from their own impetus and desires), or you could choose a new group of peers for this part of your life.

Again, however, we are brought back to the decision of telling your friends about your secret identity or not. It can be complicated, but not impossible. Also, if you have chosen to take a partner (which I recommend), you will at least have the guidance of one other who understands the road you walk.

With a secret identity (as opposed to a public one), you also cut down on the time you have to actually be a SuperHero. It's a fun job once you get your powers, and honestly you may not want to give that up. I certainly don't want to.

There is of course another option. It's a hybrid of the two. Go public, but only to your chosen inner circle. It's the best of both worlds, with few drawbacks. It does have at least one downside however: lack of publicity.

• THE MARKET AS MASTER

As you may know, much of what it takes to become successful in one field is directly translatable into what it takes to become successful in another field. There are certain precepts and actions that are accepted because they work. Marketing and branding, as just an example, are two such concepts.

Like any business, if you expect to get clients, earn the public trust, and spread word of your exploits, you will need to be well marketed, and even better branded. I won't get too deep into these concepts in this book. There isn't space, for one. For another, it wouldn't do the topic justice. There are entire companies who do this job. You won't get everything from a few paragraphs.

What I will say is this: you will always be better marketed when you can pull out all the stops. Having an identity that you must conceal, may prevent that from happening. There is an exception to this: Sometimes the public thrives on mystery. What is key here is that you will be among the first to brand, and promote, truly super heroism in the workplace and as such you gain a major market advantage.

• SOME ASSEMBLY REQUIRED

From here we move into what it takes to assemble your SuperHero identity. The question of covert or overt can still be resolved later if you choose. This is because much of this section will apply to either answer. You still would need a name, a slogan, the aforementioned marketing and branding, etc. This being the case, we will spend a minute or two on instruction about some of these pieces and also on creating your identity in general.

The easiest way to start is by leveraging what we already have. Since I know you have been following along and completing each of the exercises (You have, haven't you?) it's safe to say that you are now equipped with: (Check off the ones you have done.)

    ❍ A MISSION STATEMENT

    ❍ A VISION STATEMENT

    ❍ A KNOWLEDGE OF WHAT TYPE OF SUPERHERO YOU DESIRE TO BE

    ❍ A MYTHOLOGY

    ❍ A MORAL CODE

    ❍ POSSIBLY A PARTNER

This means you already know what type of situations you will face in your struggle and with whom you will face them (if anyone). If you can remember back to the beginning of the book, to that exercise you did with the ringing phone, you will also remember what it is that truly motivates you. It was that thing you chose when you were mentally put into fight-or-flight mode. Subliminally, this means you fought for it. You must really want it then.

You also know how far you are willing to go to resolve a problem. You knew that before this book however. It's called conflict resolution, and it's an important life skill.

If you combined all of those areas, you should have been able to write your mythology fairly easily... and that's excellent! With each thing in mind then, your marketing message should come out fairly easily as well. Talk about what you do... how amazing you are, etc. Keep it catchy but direct. Things like your marketing message, and your mission statement, will be used with members of the press (and the general public) quite often, so make them great!

• READ THE LABEL

As to the logo, this is more than just something for the chest plate of your costume. Even if you aren't going to be using a costume, you will still need a logo to represent you. Remember, since not everyone speaks your native tongue, an easily recognizable symbol will go a long way towards familiarity. Uses include letterhead, signage, and t-shirts for your fans. You will have fans, won't you?

Also, print your logo on card stock as well. You'll be glad you did. The idea here isn't just for a business card. In fact, although business cards have their place for a SuperHero, what I have in mind is a little cooler. The idea is basically like a calling card (not the telephone kind).

By calling card, I mean that it can serve as a little reminder to the person you have just rescued. It can serve as a warning to evil-doers. It can have an emergency contact number on it for those who may one day be in distress. What it really is, however, is a way to spread your legend to the world. Make it sleek. Keep it small. It isn't a business card so don't treat it like one.

Your logo will also figure prominently in your advertising. Yes: advertising. The world has to know somehow. If all of your ads contain your logo, you send a more consistent message to the world. You send stability. For a SuperHero, that's a primary trait.

• WHAT'S IN A NAME

Also to be included in your marketing is your name. This is obvious I know. I just like covering all of my bases. Maybe you had an idea as soon as you finished the initial phone call. Some do, some don't. Some just need it coaxed out of them. Honestly, if you're the name-taking type then your mind already knows it. It may just take a little explication.

If you do want one, and don't have one in mind already, don't worry, you can still brainstorm now. Take a look at your mythology first and foremost. This is helpful because a properly written mythology is more than just a record. In our case, it is an action-plan as well. And not just any plan—this one came directly from your wildest dreams, in that most optimistic part of you, deep inside yourself. The one that knows you can accomplish anything.

When you wrote that, you outlined things that you would go and do. Things you wanted to experience; things you wanted to achieve. Once you achieve them, you know you will become a completely different person.

So I ask you: Once you complete all of your training, and survive all of your adventures, by what name will you be called then? When people look up at you... what is it they will think?

If you have not yet completed the exercises and written them down, however, you may have to take a different route to get there. Maybe take a look at your support group. How do they know you? In what form? What name might they suggest for you?

Another alternative, in case these haven't worked yet, is to look at the mission and vision statements you created earlier. Done right, they outline your ideal mental path and focus. They also explain to you what has to happen for you to be a success. Align yourself along this road. Project your ideas forward along your timeline. What name would you choose for yourself now?

If you want to wait on choosing a name for your SuperHero self though, you can. In fact, quite possibly the most obvious way of finding a name for yourself (and therefore easiest), is to base your SuperHero name around the super-powers you will eventually choose. That's perfectly fine. It's also quite clever since the best way to capture the public eye is with simplicity. Use a meme or a mnemonic device that ties your name to what you do. You will definitely be noticed, and more importantly: remembered. So yes, you may want to name it after your super-powers... and by the way, that will work nicely since that part of the book will be coming up quite soon, in Part III.

• OH THE COLORS

The last little bit here is the visual make-up of your imagined self. This would be like a giant illustration of your entire persona. Intimidated? Don't be. It's as easy as everything else has been here. Don't worry. Seriously, go ahead and try, just draw a picture of it, right now. Please. Go ahead.

What's that? You say you can't draw? Just go to HeroMachine.com and do your design process over there. Take at least 3 hours on this project and then print it out. I think you will be quite pleased with the results. But remember, the time and focus you spend here is the entire key to this working.

My SuperHero Elements:

NAME: ....

LOGO: ....

COLORS: ....

COSTUME: YES | NO   *(circle one)*

HERO MACHINE COMPLETED: YES | NO

MARKETING MESSAGE:

....

....

....

....

....

Ok, you have just created your SuperHero identity. Now let's move forward and get you some super-powers!

Before you go on, however, may I suggest that since this is basically the last chapter in Part I that you look over the previous chapters, review what you have written and ensure that the understanding you have of your SuperHero self is unwavering. You don't have to understand all SuperHeroes, just yourself.

Remember, you will need a strong foundation to make it through SuperHero Boot Camp. This will be an incredible challenge, if you apply yourself.

Now as you may expect, this next half of the book is where we get a little tougher on you. You have finished with theory and have done all the required reading so, after a brief intermission, the hard work will begin. Expect the verbiage to change and the writing style to get more terse. But on the brighter side you can also expect it to cut right to the heart of things. I will not be mincing words here. I will be pushing you to overcome years of sedentary behavior. As you may have been anticipating... you are now poised to become... a SuperHero!

Special Pull-Out Section

A FIRST LOOK AT THE COMIC MANIFESTO

A First Look at the Comic Manifesto

Welcome to your very first comic book! I'll bet you didn't think you'd have a featured spot so soon did you? Well SuperHeroes do not mess around so I figured we'd just jump in. Now, in order to fill up the pages of this exciting tome, we obviously need a bunch of content. And obviously the best place to look for content is in the work that we've already done.

Let's take a few minutes right now and gather up all the exercises you've completed so far. Now this is designed to be completed online at TheSuperHeroMovement.com and I've created a special place there for you to do so. These pages however are just designed to give you one cohesive place in which to keep all of your new SuperHero information until you get a chance to go to the website and complete it. This will make it easier to refer back to when that time comes.

And now... without further ado...

Welcome friends, to your new... Comic Manifesto.

Comic Manifesto

IT'S YOU! IN THE THING! YEAH!

With my apologies to The Beatles for the title of this section, I now proclaim:

Attention all SuperHero trainees, you may now begin the transfer all of your completed SuperHero information in to the categories below.

Fill in the parts that you have for now. The other pages can get added later, after you have completed their corresponding chapters and have done their exercises.

YOU ANSWERED THE CALL FOR HELP

(First and second exercises, front of the book)

Consider again the reason that you were being called in this urgent matter of life or death, and answer it below.

....

If this person does need your help, the help of a SuperHero in fact, then tell us:

WITH WHAT? ANSWER IT NOW.

....

....

....

Now that you have this idea firmly in your mind—who is calling you? Is it some special team? A secret organization? The government? A non-profit? In the deep corners of your mind, you already know.

WHO IS IT THAT NEEDS YOU FOR THIS MISSION?
Write it down:

....

YOUR SUPERHERO PLEDGE

*I, _____ , pledge to undertake this task of becoming
a SuperHero. I understand this will require me to complete the
exercises in each chapter with great attention to detail. I will put
great care into designing every part of my SuperHero persona and
in return, be rewarded with everything I want for my future self.*

Signed _____

Date _____

YOUR COMPLETE COMMITMENT TO YOUR MISSION

BELIEVE ➡ KNOW ➡ DO ➡ BE

These are the four steps; this is the process of true commitment. When you truly
commit, you will be ready to ascend. The steps are simple, but they are not easy.

What is it in your life that deserves this sort of commitment?
What speaks to you, drives you, incites passion? What is so
powerful for you that you would dedicate your life to it?

....

....

③ YOUR SUPERHERO TYPE

**AFTER CAREFULLY CONSIDERING THE 3 CATEGORIES
I CHOOSE TO BE A:**

....

THIS IS BECAUSE:

....

....

4

YOUR SUPERHERO ALIGNMENT

ALIGNMENT POSSIBILITIES

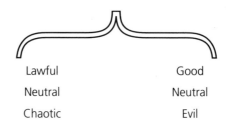

Lawful	Good
Neutral	Neutral
Chaotic	Evil

YOUR SUPERHERO VALUES

VALUES I UPHOLD	NEUTRAL	VALUES I OPPOSE

A STATEMENT ABOUT YOUR BELIEF SYSTEM

I CAN SUMMARIZE MY MORAL ALIGNMENT BY SAYING:

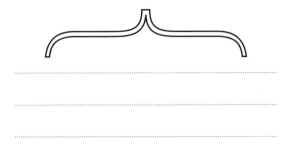

....

....

....

⑤ YOUR SUPERHERO MISSION STATEMENT

MY MISSION:

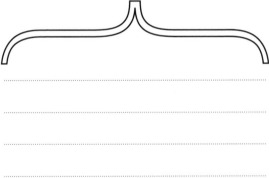

....

....

....

....

THE MISSION STATEMENT TEST:

Say your mission statement aloud. How does it feel? Does it suit you? Does it call you to action? Does it feel powerful? Is it a solid direction to your future? Does it give you an idea of what to do next (both at work and at home)?

MY VISION

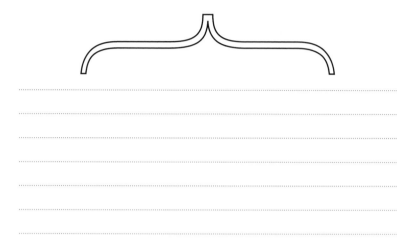

....

....

....

....

....

....

....

6

YOUR SUPERHERO TOMBSTONE

MY EPITAPH:
....
....
....

YOUR SUPERHERO MAGAZINE COVER

MAGAZINE

YOUR LIST OF SUPERHERO ADVENTURES

COOL THINGS I HAVE ALREADY DONE:	COOL THINGS I HAVE YET TO DO:
○	○
○	○
○	○
○	○
○	○
○	○

YOUR SUPER AMAZING, DREAM JOB

MY DREAM JOB:

SUPERHERO MYTHOLOGY IDEA STARTERS
(Circle One)

My Dream Job | My Adventurer's List | My Accomplishments

YOUR SUPER POWERFUL MYTHOLOGY STATEMENT

MYTHOLOGY STATEMENT EXAMPLE:
"I'm Hub McCann. I've fought in two world wars, and countless smaller ones on three continents. I've led thousands of men into battle with everything from horses and swords to artillery and tanks. I've seen the headwaters of the Nile and tribes of natives no white men had ever seen before. I've won and lost a dozen fortunes, killed many men, and loved only one woman with a passion a flea like you could never begin to understand. That's who I am."
MY MYTHOLOGY STATEMENT:

♂

YOUR SUPERHERO PARTNER STATUS

TO PARTNER, OR NOT TO PARTNER...

HERE IS MY ANSWER:

○ LONER

○ DUO

○ SIDEKICK

○ TEAM / LEAGUE   ○ FIND A TEAM / BUILD A TEAM

○ OTHER:

. . . .

POTENTIAL PARTNERS / TEAMS / TEAM MEMBERS INCLUDE:

....

....

....

YOUR SUPERHERO PERSONA:

MY SUPERHERO ELEMENTS:

NAME: ....

LOGO: ....

COLORS: ....

COSTUME: YES | NO   *(circle one)*

HERO MACHINE COMPLETED: YES | NO

MARKETING MESSAGE:

....

....

....

....

....

YOUR SUPERHERO LOGO

MY SUPERHERO LOGO:

YOUR SUPERHERO IMAGE

MY HEROMACHINE.COM PICTURE

⑩ YOUR SUPERHERO INTENTION

I WILL BECOME:

11

YOUR SUPERHERO CORE POWERS

MY CORE POWER CHECKLIST

- ○ Speed Reading
- ○ Reflex Training System
- ○ Running/Athleticism
- ○ Do it Now
- ○ CPR/First Aid
- ○ Time-Management
- ○ Volunteerism
- ○ Master of Class
- ○ Advanced Memory Power
- ○ Meditation
- ○ Neuro-Linguistic Programming

12

YOUR PRIMARY SUPERHERO POWERS AND ABILITIES

MY SUPER-POWER CHECKLIST

FREELANCER	FREE-RUNNER	FLYER
○ Conversational Hypnotism	○ Tactical Driving	○ Remote Viewing
○ Parental Powers	○ Martial Arts	○ Lucid Dreaming
○ Learn a Language	○ Small Arms Training	○ Out-of-Body Experiences
○ Public Speaking	○ Knife Throwing	○ Precognition
○ Human Lie Detection	○ Lock-Picking	○ Quantum Healing
○ Stealth	○ Survival Skills	○ Traditional Chinese Medicine
	○ Police Academy Course	○ Shibumi
	○ Gadgetry	
	○ Parkour	

13

YOUR SUPERHERO MENTOR

MY MENTOR(S):

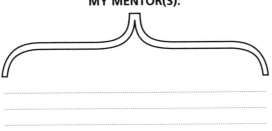

....

....

....

YOUR HIGHLY-SPECIALIZED SUPERHERO TRAINING

MY SPECIALIZED CLASSES AND SCHOOLS:

....

....

....

....

14

YOUR SUPERHERO TOOLS AND WEAPONS

MY TOOLS OF THE SUPERHERO TRADE

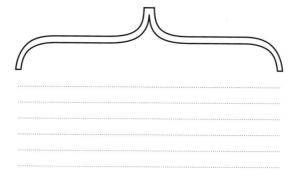

....

....

....

....

....

....

15

THE ELEMENTS OF YOUR SECRET LAIR

MY SECRET LAIR CHECKLIST

○ Secret Entrance

○ Inner Sanctum

○ Hall-of-Fame

○ Most Wanted List

○ Gadget Gallery

○ Danger Room

○ Offshore Accounts

THE HIGHLIGHTS OF YOUR SECRET LAIR

SECRET ENTRANCE DETAILS	INNER SANCTUM DETAILS	HALL-OF-FAME DETAILS
GADGET GALLERY DETAILS	DANGER ROOM DETAILS	OFFSHORE ACCOUNTS DETAILS

YOUR FUTURE SUPERHERO ACQUISITIONS

MY MOST WANTED LIST

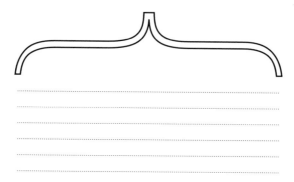

TIME MANIPULATION MAP
(Website)

MY SUPERHERO SCHEDULE

Priorities:

Hours Free per day:

16
YOUR MISSION CONTROL STATUS

MY FIRST SUPERHERO MISSION

People I have enrolled:

- ○ ....
- ○ ....
- ○ ....
- ○ ....
- ○ ....
- ○ ....

My Quest:

....

....

....

....

....

....

17

YOUR COLLATERAL SUPERHERO TRAINING

MY SUPPLEMENTAL TRAINING

- ☑ Improv class (to think on my feet)
- ☑ Learn to play Go (for strategy)
- ○ Gymnastics class (as a fitness adjunct)
- ○ ....
- ○ ....
- ○ ....

18

YOUR BATTLE AGAINST THE DARK SIDE

MY KRYPTONITE	MY ARCH-ENEMY
MY MOST CHALLENGING FOES	MY PLAN OF ATTACK

⓳
YOUR SUPERHERO LEGACY

MY LEGACY CHECKLIST	A STATEMENT OF MY LEGACY
◯ Charitable Foundation?	....
◯ Drug-Free School ?	....
◯ Successful Business ?	....
◯	....
◯	....
◯	....

(PART II)

⇩

SuperHero Boot Camp

The Only Easy Day Was Yesterday

A FIRST LOOK AT TRAINING YOUR CORE

A First Look at Training Your Core

First you must train the mind. Next you must train the body. Then you must train the spirit. The reason you must do this is simple. You are weak.

The steps of your training will be clear and direct. You are to follow them in order. The reason you must first train the mind is because if the mind is not disciplined then you will not succeed. The mind must be strong enough to carry out your wishes. It is yours to command as are all of your other weapons and soldiers. Use it appropriately, or fail.

When the mind is ready to command the rest of your considerable might, you will know. You have always known.

The body is the next tool in your arsenal, until you are more ready. When the mind is more powerful, you won't even need the body. You will grow more powerful, as will your tools. Until that time you will use what you have open to you. For you, then, the body is an appropriate next step. Eventually you will outshine this simple instrument however, and these steps will prepare you.

Next, you are commanded to train the spirit. By spirit, it is meant to commit with the whole of your being. It is your focus, your energy, your pure, inner force. There are many people who speak of an inner force but haven't the ability to truly harness it. You must learn to harness your spirit. It is a fierce and powerful tool. With it you will control many. You will control entire worlds. This is not to be taken lightly.

These tools: your mind, body, and spirit, are powerful. They are in fact the best you have ever seen... when you know what it is that you are seeing. For now, use the body and use it well. On this plane of existence it will serve you as you expect. There is much more meaning in this than may meet the eye.

YOUR TRAINING WILL PROGRESS AS FOLLOWS:

You must begin with breathing. This is not a function of the body; this is a function of the mind. You must always breathe by pulling your air-flow through your stomach: there is a great center of power there. Find the exact center of your body. Breathe from, and focus on, this point. It will circulate your life force throughout. Pulling your air-flow through your stomach helps you use your lungs to their full capacity, and not just taking shallow breaths from the tops of them. Ideally though, you will be breathing with your entire body.

Imagine your oxygen literally rushing into you from every direction, with each tremendous breath you take; feel it coming in from all sides of you. It should come up from the ground through your feet and fill your body to almost bursting. Air should pour into you from in front of, behind, and around, your torso. Feel it come into your whole body with your breaths. Imagine that when you breathe in powerfully, it comes down from heaven, right into you, through your head. Your air, your oxygen, your very life force, pours into you from all around. Breathe it in deeply. You will yawn from the extra intake at first. Breathe with all of you.

Breathing begins as a function of the mind (not body) in that you have been conditioned since birth to breathe improperly. It will take the full power of the mind to overcome such an automatic habit. You will eventually turn this into muscle-memory. This is your goal, though it will take much in the way of training and fortitude.

Breathe with your entire body. Breathe as though you were breathing in the entire earth. Breathe it up from the ground and into you and then thrust it back beneath you from whence it came. And do it all very slowly and controlled.

Do this and you will achieve much power.

When the mind has become strong enough to always breathe in this most proper way, then and only then is it strong enough to move on to other tasks. Do not stop until you have mastered this ability to breathe in the prescribed manner. It may take days; it may take weeks. When you are breathing in this way, you may read further.

Now that you have accomplished this, you may take on more challenges. This is a matter of discipline. If you cannot achieve this task, then you will not be successful in the other tasks. Do not waste your time. It will be for naught. Discipline will carry you when all else has fled your body.

What you are doing is training your mind to understand that there is nothing outside its grasp. You are training your mind to do your bidding, no matter the cost, no matter the preconceived notion. You must understand the depth of this before you proceed. To do otherwise will prove disastrous.

You will have the power you seek, but you will not have it without making this journey.

You will learn the illusion of limitation. You will find all limitation to be self-imposed. It has always been so. Doubting this statement leads one astray. There are those who understand. They have achieved the power you have only begun to seek. They have made much of this realm for they can now unlock its secrets.

For clarity, then: your limitation is self-created. This understanding alone will allow you to overcome many obstacles, if you can but harness it. Do not accept the artificial limit.

Now then, if you have learned to breathe in the very Earth upon which you stand, to harness the power of life around you, then we are ready to proceed.

Next you will gain the power of focus. This power of focus is not only "of" the mind, this "is" the mind. You are what you are because you have become that focus. To be more clear: to exist on this planet means you are an instance of focus. Nothing more.

There is a being much more powerful than your current human body from which you have sprung. It is this that has created you here. This being has decided to focus on this existence. You, in effect, have chosen to focus on being you at this very moment. If this sounds too very esoteric, then leave it be. Some will understand; others will gain this knowledge elsewhere. Either way, move on.

The power of focus can easily be developed. Do not make it a battle. Make nothing a battle and you will always win. You are not a thing in progress... be complete.

You will now learn to discipline your mind to be completely aware of its surroundings. Close your eyes for 10 seconds right now and re-create all the elements in the room around you. You have ten seconds. Be as complete as you can in what you recall. Do this once an hour.

As a beginner, you may stop at only 5 seconds. This must eventually be expanded however, to a full 10 seconds of exacting detail. With practice you will become adept. You will always know what and who is around you at any moment. You will be well on your way to gaining your first powers. Master your core. The rest will come.

This is all a matter of focus. You are training to improve the power of your mind. Observation and recall are important in this. This practice can be done anywhere. While you are driving your car, at any random point, recall the last three cars that you passed on your right. What type were they? What color were they? Were there people inside? How many? For now, just keep this practice simple and quick. Over time you will come to strengthen this ability.

Next you will learn to detect the truth of men's actions and statements. You can do this in many ways. The first thing to understand about this is that, on some level, you already know the truth, and therefore can already see through them.

Body language and tone will count for a full 93% of a person's communication. This means that only 7% is left to the specific words. Therefore, as I have said, on a sub-conscious level you already know. Learn to tap into this.

There are of course many signs. There are the eyes. If a person looks to the right (your left) and up, then they are creating a story, not remembering one. If they look to the opposite side, (your right, their left) then, this shows that they are remembering, not fabricating. This is true in the majority of cases, although some people will have these sides reversed in them. You must learn to assess the difference. You can do this with test questions (questions to which you already know the answer). Test the subject. Watch their reactions. Think it through. You'll get it without much difficulty.

Also, there is the pupil dilation. Watch for a person's pupils to shrink when they lie to you. That is of course unless they have developed such a comfort with lying that they have no problems with it at all. Again, you must be diligent in your learning. But understand, if you are conscious, then you will already know. Just be sure you are sufficiently alert.

Look next to the person's breathing patterns and heart-rate. Have those indicators accelerated? Why would this happen, unless they were afraid that they would get caught at something; perhaps lying. Again, use these guides only as secondary information, since you must learn to rely on your own innate judgment first. These are but markers.

Look also to their tone. Is a person pleading in their dialogue with you? Are they adamant? Are they enraged? What emotion is coming across, and why?

" ...your limitation is self-created. Do not accept the artificial limit.

Finally, having covered these areas, you may now look at their words. Have they a well thought out statement? What does this indicate to you? There is much to this entire process, but these things should play second to your own intuition.

As a final note on this subject, you must always come from a place of honesty in your dealings with others. If you are to see things clearly, then you must always do this. Your vision will be limited otherwise.

This completes your instruction on the training of the mind.

Now to the training of the body. This will be either easy or difficult. It is your choice. If you want it to be hard, then it will be. Again, all limitation is self-limitation. Make this choice and move forward. Easy or difficult is a fool's concern. Take the lesson and advance, whichever road you choose.

The first step in training the body is to check on the training of the mind. If you have completed your first lessons then this first task has already been completed. We will put it now to the test. Sprint until you are winded. If this takes you one minute, then stop after one. If this takes you twenty seconds, then stop after twenty seconds. Once you are winded, check your breathing. Are you breathing slowly and controlled from your stomach? Are you breathing from your center? Or perhaps only from the tops of your lungs? If you are not breathing properly, there is question over whether or not you have completed the other tasks.

This new concept of breathing is not a question of fitness. This is a matter of discipline. If you are bound to a wheelchair, you still can choose whether to breathe life in fully, or you can choose to take it in with shallow little gasps. The concept is the same. Breathe with your entire being. Breathe it all in—every drop. Not to do so, is to squander it. So breathe!

If you have not passed this test, go back to the beginning of this section and begin again. Your very future depends on it. Once you can maintain your breathing strategy while winded, it is time to move on.

The next task in training your body is your posture. Though you may consider this to be still a function of the mind, and therefore out of place in the body section, it is wise to remember that everything in the body is dependent on the mind anyway. Your goal here is still muscle memory. Yes, the mind brings you the discipline... use it to now train your muscles.

Moving on from this (assuming you have gone back and finished the exercises of the mind), and training you more on the body, your posture is critical. Your physical power will derive from your posture. Maintain it at all costs.

This is to be taken metaphorically as well as literally. When you sit, sit up straight. When you stand, you must stand proud. Your chest must be out. Your posture alone is enough to sway many a foe.

To your enemies, the world is a desolate place waiting only to dash their hopes and crush their dreams. They are always expecting to be defeated. You will assist them in this endeavor by becoming fate's agent. Keep your posture strong. Proud and strong, or not at all.

Your posture will change your eating habits. It will change your peer group. It will change your goals and will increase your success in meeting those goals. It will do all this for you... but you must maintain your SuperHero posture always. Stand proud.

Rise early. From this day forward, wherever possible, you will see the sun rise. You will awake before dawn and witness this day coming into creation. When you are powerful enough you will see how much of it you created. Until then, you will rise to see it as only a spectator. Rise then! Rise!

If you do this every day, you will achieve success in life. This is not up for discussion. Become the power. Become the focus. Show it in your walk. Show it in your posture. Stand proud and strong. Arise before the dawn. Take this world by storm. It is your destiny.

As we are still training the body in this phase, you will next learn to increase your physical strength. There is a mental key to this physical task. Give yourself the permission to make these mental changes manifest on a physical level and it will be so.

Commit to becoming stronger. It matters not what exercise routine you pursue, only that you choose one and pursue it with a zealous fervor. If you will run, run. If you will become incredibly strong, capable of lifting hundreds of pounds, then do so. Whatever you choose, attack it and make it who you are. Again, your exercise routine is irrelevant. It is only your commitment to it that matters.

If you are incapable of choosing your own exercise routine, one will be presented to you momentarily. If you have one already, use it.

For those who choose to become the physical hero, you must improve your agility as well as your reflexes. Do not focus only on increasing strength. Strength must not be overlooked of course, but do not neglect the other areas either, while in this pursuit.

Commit to this physical improvement every day. Maintain your breathing. Swim, if you are capable. It will increase much in you. Improve the strength and capacity of your heart and your lungs in any way you see fit. The method matters not. It is only your commitment that matters. Strive, every day. Reach your goals, every day.

Pay much attention to what you eat. Again, the choices you make may stem from your own knowledge or from others. This is largely irrelevant. Trust your instincts. Pay attention to what you consume, or be victim to it consuming you.

It does not take much to surpass the common man. This is why they are so common. Strive now, for there are many who will not.

Having completed this section on the body, you may move forward to the next phase. There will be more in-depth body work for those who are seeking it later. I will offer you a physical routine that appears deceptively simple, but only when you are ready. Until that time you must complete the training you have just been taught. When you are ready, you may continue on to the next section.

You must now focus on training your spirit. You will find this to be a simple matter of commitment. Unfortunately, however, you may not yet understand commitment. Do not pay lip-service to this ideal. Become it. Identify what it is that you will become... not what you may become, or what you want to become... only what you will become.

Indeed, I challenge you to answer it now, if you can. What will you become? If you must, then write it here beginning with the words:

"I will become _____ ." But whatever you do, decide now what it is and grab hold of it. Commit to realizing your vision in as much detail as possible... right now.

Once you have done this, maintain it, and you will have everything you have ever wanted. This is a fact. There are those who have it all. They discovered it and then never let it go. Do not merely pursue—you must grab! You must achieve!

It is always, in every venture, that the most committed will win. It is always thus. Luck plays a factor only when luck is created. Where you commit with the intention—or where you fight with the spirit—the sword will inevitably follow. Place your focus and your will in that place, and then overwhelm and absolutely crush your odds. It is the Way.

You now understand the core of what you must do. You now understand what you must become. Mind, Body, Spirit. These three in harmony will always bring you success... and more than that... will make you into a hero; the greatest hero... a SuperHero.

This is to be the training of your core.

Success in your training will take planning and scheduling. It will take dedication. If you are ready, we will begin.

You will rise at dawn. While you are watching the sunrise you will practice only your breathing and your posture. This is a simple matter. Simply focus your eyes to take in more than they usually do while breathing deeper than you normally do. Concentrate only on your breathing.

This is meditation. You must maintain this throughout the sunrise. Hold your posture. Focus the eyes on a wider area. Concentrate always on your breathing. Nothing more. This alone will prepare you for what is to come.

You will not always meditate in this way of non-movement. This is not meant to be lived as a stationary practice. It is only this way now because you are still learning. Eventually you will maintain this focus in everything you do.

Do you remember the 10-second memory drills? Have you become proficient in them? Continue your training of focus with this simple practice. Close your eyes again. What is around you now? Describe in the exacting detail to which you have become accustomed.

Ready now? There is more. Go now to your kitchen and open a cabinet. Quickly, memorize what you see there. Quickly!

Now close the cabinet. Can you recall the items? What are they? Where are they? Have you succeeded in this new exercise?

Repeat this until you are flawless. Do not stop half way. Become amazing at this. It is what we do when no-one is looking that matters. Focus and do not stop until you have perfected this skill.

Now move to your refrigerator. Again, open it. At one glance you will know everything that is contained therein. This will be true if you have become flawlessly adept at the cabinets.

After a period of one month of daily meditation, of continuous, proper breathing technique, proper posture, and one month of focused practice on your recall, you will see amazing advances in all areas of your life. All areas. This is fact. Maintain this through diligence.

SUPPLEMENTAL

Now we can circle back around and focus more on training the body. These exercises will be simple in nature. If you have a structure and workout that provides you results, then by all means, use it. This section offers you something if you don't. You will train yourself to be your best.

At this moment, when you think of being your best, you can probably only think of the limits of your human capability. This limitation has nothing to do with your true capacity. It is irrelevant. You are no longer limited to definitions imposed by the Human Race. You will in fact become one of the first members of the Super-Human Race.

You will not be alone in this. There are many who will join you. You are only guiding the way. Become a beacon for them, that they may follow in your footsteps. Show the world what they may become and you may yet free them from their bonds.

Allow them to drop the chains of human bondage that has 'til now restrained them. Free yourself from your own chains and free all of humanity with the same gesture.

You are more than what you have seen. You are more even than you have lived. Rise up with the power of flight! Elevate yourself and raise up your fellow man! Lead them from the darkness of their caves and bring them to strength; bring them to freedom!

FOR YOUR OWN PROTECTION

There are two requirements here:

➡ **1.** Consult your physician before you begin.

➡ **2.** If you are completely out of shape when you begin this, work yourself up to the point where you can comfortably move for 20 minutes without stopping. That's the only other prerequisite. It can be walking, swimming, running, jumping jacks—whatever you want. Whatever you feel most likely to be able to accomplish, simply work yourself up to 20 minutes of non-stop motion. Even if it takes you months—keep going— you will make it. When you can comfortably do this consistently, you are ready to begin.

THE FITNESS OF A SUPERHERO IN THE GUISE OF A NAVY SEAL

chinfo.navy.mil/navpalib/factfile/personnel/seals/seals.html

16 MILE A WEEK RUNNING SCHEDULE

If you need help getting started, simply try to work your way up to running for a solid 20 minutes. The distance you run does not matter. Just work towards a continuous 20 minutes of moving. Afterwards, spend as long as you need until you can comfortably join the chart below.

Weeks #1,2:	2 miles/day (you may begin even more slowly)	M/W/F
Week #3:	No running (high risk of stress fractures)	n/a
Week #4:	3 miles/day	M/W/F
Weeks #5,6:	2/3/4/2 miles	M/T/TH/F
Thereafter:	4/4/5/3 miles	M/T/Th/F

➡ STRETCHING

Stretch your muscles for 15-20 minutes before you workout. Stretch again on your days off. Stretch to tightness, not to pain; hold for 10-15 seconds. Do not bounce. Stretch every muscle in your body from the neck to the calves, concentrating on your thighs, hamstrings, chest, back, and shoulders.

➡ PYRAMID WORKOUTS

Also called Step-up/Step-downs. You can do this with any exercise. The object is to slowly build up to a goal, then build back down to the beginning of the workout. For example, say your goal is 5 pull-ups: You literally do 1 pull-up; then let go. Now rest for 15 seconds. Then you grab on and do 2 pull-ups; then let go again; etc. Repeat until you finish the chart below. This is, of course, assuming the goal of 5, mentioned above. Adjust it accordingly.

EXERCISE	NUMBER OF REPETITIONS
Pull-ups:	1,2,3,4,5,4,3,2,1
Push-ups:	2,4,6,8,10,8,6,4,2 (2x #pull-ups)
Sit-ups:	3,6,9,12,15,12,9,6,3 (3x #pull-ups)
Dips:	Same as push ups

SWIMMING SCHEDULE	
Weeks #1,2:	Swim continuously for 15 min.
Weeks #3,4:	Swim continuously for 20 min.
Weeks #5,6:	Swim continuously for 25 min.
Weeks #7,8:	Swim continuously for 30 min.
Thereafter:	Swim continuously for 35 min.

*Note: If you have no access to a pool, ride a bicycle for twice as long as you would swim. If you do have access to a pool, swim everyday.

SUPERHERO BOOT CAMP DE-BRIEFING

Ok... The rough stuff is over. Expect the verbiage to tone down again and return to be more like the language to which you may have grown accustomed.

Ever wonder how one chapter can be considered an entire section of a book? This section actually takes at least 9 weeks to complete. Conversely, almost every other chapter in this book was completed as soon as you read it (and finished a few written exercises). If you haven't gone through it... you do still own the book. Just go back and do them now.

The real secret to this book (and I am somewhat surprised that I am sharing it with you, although some of you already know this), is that you never needed this book to begin with anyway. Yes, it has valuable information, and yes if you walk the path you will become more than anyone has ever seen. But you see... that was never the key.

The key is, and always was, with you. In fact if I had it to write it all over again I may just call it Dumbo's Feather... except my marketing instincts tell me that it won't sell.

Listen, I am about to tell you how to actually see beyond all time and space in a way that has been proven, time and again, by the various governments of the world. I won't show you their studies, I will show you how to learn it yourself. I will show you that (with the proper training) you can literally leap from tall buildings without harm. You will learn things in here that, until now, you may have considered impossible. But none of it—not one letter of it—will ever work for you, until you go through all the steps yourself.

I am telling you this now, in your debriefing, so that you don't read something for five minutes, run off the edge of a cliff and have your loved ones sobbing at my door. Call it harsh, or call it common sense: don't jump off of anything that you aren't physically prepared for, and don't try anything that you haven't been trained by a professional instructor to do.

There are people who do it, and they have dedicated their lives to it. They do it, they live. A rookie does it, they may die. I have never once in this book suggested that these events be taken without forethought, care, and due diligence. Weekenders be warned. And good luck to those of you that undertake the courses of study in earnest.

PART III

Super Powers

The Heart of it All

A FIRST LOOK AT THE CORE POWERS

A First Look at the Core Powers

In this section, you will find a number of powers for you to learn. These are what I have designated as the core powers. No matter what type of SuperHero you have chosen to become, no matter what your mission is, these powers will serve you well. You must practice, and you must study to gain your mastery. However, to make life easier on you, each power is outlined with five points. Usually, these will help you to begin learning the power immediately.

It isn't meant to be an exhaustive guide, as some powers will require your outside study. It is meant, however, to get you to jump in right now. Absorb the points, learn the powers. This is necessary to become a SuperHero.

CORE POWERS

○ Speed Reading

○ Reflex Training System

○ Running/Athleticism

○ Do it Now

○ CPR/First Aid

○ Time-Management

○ Volunteerism

○ Master of Class

○ Advanced Memory Power

○ Meditation

○ Neuro-Linguistic Programming

➡ SPEED READING

This is easily one of the first skills you must master. The reason for this is simple. If you can acquire your knowledge easily and instantly, you will never be at a loss for information on your missions. You will know where to look and when. Once there, you will devour the information readily. This key unlocks many other powers. It is therefore essential.

Here are 5 key elements to this ability:

➡ **1.** Trust your instincts. You are better at this than you think you are.

➡ **2.** Read silently... directly down the center of the column. Resist the urge to scan left and right more than a few words. Go down the center.

➡ **3.** Use a guiding hand at first. As you progress this will become unnecessary.

➡ **4.** Begin with magazines and junior-high school textbooks, they are specifically designed to be read in this way (narrow columns that can be read almost straight down). Then move on to newspapers and finally novels where the sentences elongate. The beginning content is simple and it is arranged to make it easy for you. As the material progresses, so too will your skill.

➡ **5.** Keep your mind open at all costs. There is a big difference between scanning a chapter for familiarity and having a preconceived notion of what is written.

➡ REFLEX TRAINING SYSTEM

How well can you take a punch? What if you never had to find out? Hone your reflexes as if your life depended on it. One day, it just might. Make your hand-eye coordination unbeatable with the following exercises. Except for one step, they can all be done alone.

➡ **1.** Strap a Bounce-Back Ball to each wrist and then begin to throw them at increasingly faster speeds. $5.00

➡ **2.** Throw a 6-sided MD USA Reaction Ball against a brick wall at increasingly closer ranges. With a partner you can simply drop it between you and see who can instantly grab it. A 3" ball is $5.00

➡ **3.** Only after the above 2 steps have been mastered are you cleared to move forward to this step: Nerf Dart Guns. My preference is the Maverick. Have your training partner shoot this at you at increasingly closer ranges. Do not flinch. Catch the projectiles instead. (Insert the obligatory "don't shoot your eye out" phrase here.)

➡ **4.** Variations on a theme. With Bounce-Back balls you should get to the stage where you can run while performing the actions in step one. Side-step them and catch them from behind. With the dart guns you will eventually learn to slip them. This is not dodging them. This is an incredible boxing maneuver (wikihow.com). When you perform this correctly it will be similar to the moves of the Grammaton Cleric in the movie Equilibrium. Also, you must take this step only after you have learned to not flinch while catching the projectiles.

➡ **5.** The Big Leagues. After you have accomplished all of the above tasks, you are permitted to move to the next level. Heed this advice, or suffer the consequences. The next level, in this case, is a tennis court—standing in front of two Kanon Tennis Ball Machines that can be set to speeds up to 75 mph. First you will learn to catch them without flinching. Then you will learn to slip them. Eventually you will have them launched simultaneously. Then almost no one can touch you.

➡ RUNNING/ATHLETICISM

If you are looking for guidance on how to begin training your body, take up running. It trains much of your body at once, and improves your endurance. Endurance alone is a power on which SuperHeroes must rely. Your overall athleticism will greatly increase. Running is advantageous to you because it also trains your mind. It focuses your mind on every sensation your body feels and teaches you to push yourself to new limits. Become a great runner and you will become mentally and physically stronger.

If you have followed the advice in Part II, you will already be running at least 16 miles a week, and be in the best shape of your life. If you haven't, the following steps are for you.

Here is your 5-step, quick start guide to begin right this moment:

➡ **1.** Put on a pair of comfortable and supportive running shoes and some light, comfortable clothing (the only equipment you will need).

➡ **2.** Do a short 5-10 minute warm up by walking or lightly jogging. Then spend about ten minutes stretching the muscles in your arms and legs.

➡ **3.** Run on a soft surface, at a comfortable pace beginning with a period of 20 minutes (only walk if your breathing becomes greatly labored, but NEVER fully stop moving in this time). Do not worry about how fast you are going. Your goal, as a beginner, is to get your body comfortable with running without stopping. When you can run without stopping for twenty minutes, begin to increase the time you spend running in increments of five or ten minutes. You will find your speed increases naturally as you begin to get more in shape.

➡ **4.** Do a short cool-down of walking or jogging and end with a few more stretches. The stretching you do at the end of your workout is actually quite helpful because your body is warmed up after the run.

➡ **5.** Do this about 3 times a week to start. As you begin to get more comfortable with running, you can increase the number of days you run, as well as the time you spend doing your run. Alternate the strain on your body by doing a longer timed run and then following it with a shorter timed run. You can soon move into various types of speed workouts to begin honing your power.

➡ DO IT NOW

Essential to your set of core powers is developing the ability to "do it now." It is simple to learn. Whatever you want to do, or learn, or be: start this very moment. Right now. Many suffer in execution of this power. They leave desires and goals locked away in the covered boxes of their mind. They will save pursuing them for some future date that will never come. You must not fall into this trap. There is only this moment, right now, as you read these words.

Do your core exercises. Right this moment. Go to your cupboards and memorize their contents. If you have already done this in your kitchen, move on to the bathroom. If you are reading this on the train, close your eyes and practice memorizing your surroundings. You can always do something this moment. Reading will not make you a SuperHero. Only doing will, truly pursuing this task with every essence of yourself.

After this page, stop reading. Do not continue to read until you have completed this task. When you cannot be distracted by a mere book, or by any part of your daily routine, and you are always able to maintain your training at every moment, you will have gained the power of "do it now."

Once more for the readers who have not yet put this into practice:

➡ **1.** Stop reading, put down the book, and accomplish part of your training. If you have completed your training, accomplish a goal. Add to your successes by moving right now.

➡ **2.** Practice your core exercises from Chapter 10.

➡ **3.** Do this over and over again throughout your day. In making yourself do something simple and short many times a day, you will train yourself to respond to your desire to do something immediately.

➡ **4.** Purposefully interrupt tasks while training. You must learn to concentrate on something immediately and to be able to switch modes immediately.

➡ **5.** When you are no longer hypnotized by various parts of your routine, and can always motivate yourself to "do it now," you will understand this power.

➡ CPR/FIRST AID

The power to save a life is needed. This is for all SuperHeroes. You do not need to be a doctor to save the day and preserve the life of another. Sometimes the simple act of giving CPR or first aid is appropriate. Be the person that will take control of the situation, that will rush to a victim's side. As a SuperHero, you must always be in control. This power will allow you to stop death. Do not take this lightly. See the power you will hold in mastering this skill. If you choose to take this to the next level (perhaps assisting the sick will be your mission) take an EMT class. The greater your commitment to your mission, the greater the power you will hold.

Here are the 5 basics of giving CPR, in case this power is needed of you today *(http://depts. washington.edu/learncpr/quickcpr.html):*

> ➡ **1.** Check the victim for unresponsiveness and call 911 if not respond-ing. An emergency operator should be able to assist you with CPR.

> ➡ **2.** Return to the victim, tilt the head back and listen for breathing.

> ➡ **3.** If not breathing normally, coughing or moving, pinch the nose, cover the mouth with yours and blow until you see the chest rise. Give two breaths for one second each. This is not safe to perform on a baby. Be very careful.

> ➡ **4.** If the victim is still not breathing normally, coughing or moving, begin chest compressions. Push down on the chest between the nipples, pressing down about one and a half to two inches deep. Give 30 com-pressions, faster than once per second.

> ➡ **5.** Continue with two breaths and 30 pumps until help arrives.

➡ TIME-MANAGEMENT

SuperHeroes have responsibilities that mere mortals do not have. However, that doesn't mean that they are free to just show up late with some lame excuse, because they were tied up elsewhere. Being a SuperHero means not shirking some responsibilities in pursuit of others. You can learn to manage all of your tasks. You can achieve more. Allow the SuperHero within you to rise.

> ➡ **1.** See no limits. You can easily be where you need to be, and do what needs to get done, provided you have mastered the Do it Now ability. When we move, we accomplish. Do not ever decide to move to the next task—simply go. Your time is not limited. You have the same amount as everyone else: Gandhi, Branson, Oprah, Jefferson... see where they have gone, and what they have done with your same minutes.

➡ **2.** Begin by establishing a list of your most important goals. Time management doesn't work because it is too subjective. Don't manage your time—manage your priorities. If you understand your goals, if you have made your plans, attend to them. Leave the other things behind. Always focus on your priorities and you will succeed.

➡ **3.** Once you have your list of goals laid out (from step 2), write down the hours of the day that are absolutely booked and not flexible (e.g. sleep, or maybe work). When you have added up all the mandatory hours subtract that number from 24 to see how many free hours you have left. Now take your goals and break them down into separate categories based on where they best fit; group them. For example: work/writing a novel/home life/SuperHero training. This makes 4 categories (or goals, or priorities, etc.) that are important to you. These 4 can be thought of as your mini-days, or mortal days.

➡ **4.** Use your new data to create a SuperHero Schedule. When done right, those four mortal days all coexist peacefully within just one of your SuperHero days. Now divide the number of free hours you have by the number of mortal days you are setting up. So in the example above if you had 8 hours free after sorting out all of your hours in step 3, then you would have 2 hours to give to each category (8 divided by 4 = 2). If you only had 4 hours free each day, then you would only allocate 1 hour for each day (4 divided by 4 = 1), etc.

➡ **5.** Next, decide before you go to sleep what 1 or 2 things you would like to accomplish for each mortal day that you have set up for tomorrow. So, for this example, perhaps you would write an outline for your novel, train your reflexes for your SuperHero training, take the family to a movie, exercise, set up a private writing area to use at home, etc. Once you know what the 2 priorities are for each mini day (or mortal day), just match them up with free time you have available from the chart you made in step 3 and then have at it. I have found that some things will take longer than you expect, so plan accordingly, and be open to trial and error until you get the hang of it. The good news is that each day you will now be moving forward on all of your goals simultaneously.

➡ VOLUNTEERISM

Become a volunteer. There is great power in donating your time to reach out to others. This must be done with purest intention. If you are only doing it to say that you have volunteered, do not do it. It will only waste your time. Remember, you must always act from a place of honesty. Don't lie to yourself about your purpose for volunteering. As such, decide what is valuable for you. Use volunteerism as a means to promote your ideals and values in the world. Consider the work of the Peace Corps for laboring overseas or AmeriCorps for your efforts at home. Choose your level of involvement, but no matter what, you must choose to be effective. You are privileged to hold the information you do in your hands. Spread it to others; show what they are capable of as well.

Here are five steps to making significant change through volunteerism:

➡ **1.** Determine your purpose for volunteering. What change do you want to affect in the world? Align it with your mission and vision statements from Chapter 5.

➡ **2.** Search Internet sites like www.volunteermatch.com, www.peacecorps.gov, bunac.org, www.idealist.org and conduct your own volunteering research. See what's out there!

➡ **3.** Search for opportunities that match your purpose for volunteering.

➡ **4.** Establish a true dedication to the cause you choose and set aside regular blocks of time for the opportunity you choose.

➡ **5.** Commit to the people you are helping, commit to what you are signing up for, commit to affecting change.

➡ BE A MASTER OF CLASS

Be suave. Be debonair. This is about acting with style. If you master the power of finesse, you will execute your powers not only flawlessly, but with a unique flair. Make this part of your identity, make it one of your trademarks. Don't be James Bond, be YOU. But do it with sophistication and charm. Your confidence will gain you much notice, just in mastering this one power. Learn the rules. Know the formalities. You will blend into any social situation you encounter, and you will attract attention with your mastery.

Here are five steps to basic table etiquette (RealSimple.com), so you may begin practicing this moment:

➡ **1.** Place your napkin on your lap as soon as you sit down; do not leave it on the table until the food comes or until you need to use it.

➡ **2.** Smaller forks are for salads and starters, bigger forks for entrees. The bigger, round spoon is for soup. Dessert cutlery is usually set near the top of the plate. It will usually be a spoon, but a fork may be placed as part of the dessert cutlery as well.

➡ **3.** Use the glass set on your right side and the bread plate on your left. If there is more than one glass set at your place, the smaller is usually for water, while the larger is for wine.

➡ **4.** Do not put utensils you have started using on the table top. Instead, rest them on your plate when you are not eating. When you are finished eating, place your cutlery at an angle across your plate, facing up. Pointing the cutlery at the person opposite to you is considered an ancient sign of aggression.

➡ **5.** Always act with politeness, graciousness, and make others feel at ease (especially if mistakes in etiquette are made). Ladies served first is the traditional rule in dining, though many consider this antiquated.

➡ ADVANCED MEMORY POWER

This is connected to the lessons on observation that you have learned in Part II. If you were diligent with that practice, you will see this as just an extension. Your mind wasn't only being trained to observe, but to record and recall as well. This is why these lessons must be done in order. By now, your mind has been trained to grasp an entire picture at a glance. On the streets this will serve you well.

Therefore, here are your 5 keys to unlocking this ability:

➡ **1.** You must include all of your senses in order to store a solid memory. This will take practice. The more cues you use to store it, the more keys you will have to retrieve it. Look for the sights, smells, sounds, everything you can about a scene that is evolving in front of you.

➡ **2.** Don't store just an image frozen in time. A moving picture, a completed scene, this will be recalled better later because you are more invested in it. You're not just bored by a still image.

➡ **3.** You must do this holistically; use the whole brain. Your IMAGINATION creates the complete picture, and then your LOGICAL side creates an association to find a place to keep it until you need it.

➡ **4.** Stimulate your mind while it is in the act. Make everything you are trying to remember as vivid as possible. Use great symbols and strong associations.

➡ **5.** Remember the example of a photographic memory: if you have a picture in front of you, you can always go back to it for any details you missed before. Yours will be even better because you have the moving picture that activates all of the senses.

➡ MEDITATION

I have spoken already about meditation. It is valuable because it gives you power over the mind. You will need this on your mission. I have spoken about when, where, and even how you must perform this. For some, this was enough and they have begun their mental journey. If you have not yet begun we offer you this one, final chance.

Use these 5 keys to meditation and find the silence you seek.

➡ **1.** Perform your meditation as the sun rises. It will instill you with the power of the new day. Do this every morning.

➡ **2.** Stand in the posture of the SuperHero you wish to be. This will be the day as you create it. Stand strong and proud so that the mere sight of you will inspire others. The SuperHero does not cower. The SuperHero does not slack or slouch. Hold your position firm, with a full chest and a clear mind.

➡ **3.** Allow your eyes to focus wider than they normally do. Take in more than you normally would. Expand your vision to encompass the limits of your peripheral vision. Surpass it. See everything around you while holding your eyes steady. Now, relax them in this position, maintaining this wider-than-normal field of view.

➡ **4.** Breathe deeper than you normally do. Breathe deeper and breathe slowly. Breathe much slower, in fact, then you normally would.

➡ **5.** Clear your mind. Focus only on your breathing. Nothing else. If thoughts should come, you must remember: you are the sky. They are but passing clouds. Focus only on your breathing.

➡ NEURO-LINGUISTIC PROGRAMMING

This is a clear and scientifically-based method for learning the intricacies of the human mind. If you can understand this well enough, you will be able to control not only your interactions with others, but also their outcomes and actions as well. This is a fact. By and large, people walk around in a trance and the SuperHero may sometimes need to use this to their advantage. Control your outcomes.

NLP offers a huge arena of study. Here are 5 starter points to give you an idea of what to next explore.

➡ **1.** Match and Mirror others to gain rapport. NLP techniques will not work otherwise. Once **you are in AMAZING rapport**, anchor this feeling by gently sliding the fingertip of your right pinkie across the back of your left pinkie finger. Only anchor the most intense feelings you can create.

➡ **2.** Control your state. A SuperHero chooses their emotions and actions carefully. **You always feel Fantastic!** Use a phrase that will help cultivate this state in you and then, slide an anchor onto the back of your left ring finger, using the fingertip from your right ring finger.

➡ **3.** Be in Cause, not in Effect. Don't blame others. You have created your own situation—always. You are not late because of the traffic; you are late by your own choosing. Feel powerful knowing that you create literally everything around you. Everything—**You are tremendously powerful.** Then slide an anchor onto the back of your left middle finger, using the fingertip of your right middle finger.

➡ **4.** Tap into Accelerated Learning techniques: Know that you easily can; Relax; Map out the information; Read it dramatically; Listen to calming music while studying; add fun & games and you will learn as easily and quickly as a child. When **you know you can learn effortlessly at any moment**, feel this sensation in you completely, and then slide an anchor onto the back of your left index finger, using the fingertip of your right index finger.

➡ **5.** Slide only one anchor onto the back of each finger and **you will have access to these states whenever you need them.** The higher the energy you were feeling when you anchored them, the stronger this will be. Sliding an anchor into place allows you to turn up the heat at any time. The more you slide the trigger the more response you will get back. Pick the five states you want access to at any moment, place them separately with high energy, and call them when you need them, either individually or in groups.

Magnificence

A FIRST LOOK AT CHOOSING YOUR SUPER-POWERS

A First Look at Choosing Your Super-Powers

This section holds the same format of the previous chapter. There are five points on each power so you may begin to understand and learn each one. These powers are more oriented to the needs of each SuperHero type. However, I still suggest you read the whole chapter through. Depending on your mission as a SuperHero, you may find powers outside of the type you have chosen to aid you in your quest. Take from this what you need. As your SuperHero identity is becoming more clearly defined, you should know exactly what purpose this chapter will serve for you. You are a SuperHero. Everything is your tool, you must use everything to serve your mission.

THE POWERS

FREELANCER	FREE-RUNNER	FLYER
○ Conversational Hypnotism	○ Tactical Driving	○ Remote Viewing
○ Parental Powers	○ Martial Arts	○ Lucid Dreaming
○ Learn a Language	○ Small Arms Training	○ Out-of-Body Experiences
○ Public Speaking	○ Knife Throwing	○ Precognition
○ Human Lie Detection	○ Lock-Picking	○ Quantum Healing
○ Stealth	○ Survival Skills	○ Traditional Chinese Medicine
	○ Police Academy Course	○ Shibumi
	○ Gadgetry	
	○ Parkour	

THE POWERS OF THE FREELANCER

Conversational Hypnotism

Parental Powers

Learn a Language

Public Speaking

Human Lie Detection

Stealth

➡ CONVERSATIONAL HYPNOTISM

It is absolutely possible to place someone quickly in a deep trance by using simple conversation. You of course, will start out with a light trance and then can move to deepen it as you like. To the SuperHero even the slightest pauses and hesitations can be valuable. It can also be helpful to change a person's way of thinking (you may need them on your side). For the creative SuperHero the uses here are clearly endless. Imagine being able to have someone unconscious in seconds.

Below are the 5 steps, in order, that you will need to learn in order to use this power effectively.

➡ **1.** Establish Rapport. Connect to the person. Relax in order to help them relax. Establish a fun, easy, and most importantly, open connection. Ask lots of questions that result in a "yes" answer. The more nodding you get, the better. Stay away from negative answers.

➡ **2.** Test your rapport, and their suggestibility. This sets the stage for what is to come. You can test with things like: Hidden Language, Sleight of Mouth, or Embedded Commands. For example, "I bet those shoes make **you feel comfortable, Sarah**." or perhaps "It looked really nice, so **I will probably move in closer** to the 15th."

➡ **3.** Knock them off-balance by saying something completely nonsensical but stare directly into their eyes when you do it, and say it seriously. In fact, if you can, stare not only into their eyes, but beyond them and through them as well. Make sure the phrase makes no sense. This is the boldest step considering that the others were done so covertly, however, the more confidently you do it, the stronger the effect will be. Your confidence is everything here. Be bold and assume your success. The more brave and direct you are, the better.

➡ **4.** At this moment their mind is blank and they are now waiting for you to fill it. They are in a trance. Add your suggestions or commands right now. This must be done immediately after the off-balancing. You have maybe only a second in which to act, maybe. Add the commands or suggestions now while you still have the opportunity. If you choose not to, they will snap out of it on their own.

➡ **5.** Assuming you kept them in trance, you can now either maintain your connection, by watching for cues and indicators and acting accordingly, or you can deepen it, by adding suggestions that they breathe deeply, relax, and go further still, into a deep, deep sleep, feeling better than they have ever felt before. When you have finished you must return them to their full consciousness and leave them on a positive note, happy, and feeling great.

➡ PARENTAL POWERS

Parents have tremendous impact in their children's lives, yet many fail to make the most of this ability. This is about guidance and structure, yes, but it is also about caring and friendship. Understanding who your child is as a person can only come from spending time with them. You don't have to spend every minute with them, in fact sometimes they need a safe space of their own. But what you can do is to invest the time you do have with them wisely. They love you. Love them back.

As such, here are 5 idea-starters. Like anything else I have mentioned, this is only a start. You must pick up the ball and run with it. This is your chance to prove to your child that not only are you a SuperHero, but that you are a SuperHero for them, and them alone.

➡ **1.** Buy a book called "Wow Dad!" It's about $9.00 and has somewhere near 170 things in it that you can do with your kids anywhere. Literally anywhere: even if you are standing in line at the bank. (Wow-Dad.com)

➡ **2.** Do not underestimate the PTA. Find out about your child's school life. Get involved. Go to parent- teacher night and ask your child to introduce you to each person they know. Tell them that they introduced you fantastically, it builds them up.

➡ **3.** Goal-Playing games are like role-playing games except you and your child imagine their life as it would be with their ultimate, happy future. It is much more than the vision statement and has much more detail. With older children, have them visualize a complete day in their perfect future. Lead them along through the visualization by saying things like: "Oh really? And then after you leave the house what is your office like? Do you work alone or do you have many friends? Is your job complicated?" Questions like these can be scaled up or down depending on the intellect of the child, but it helps to establish their goals and direction in life.

➡ **4.** Mini Job-Shadowing lets the child in on your work life. Show them where you work. If you can't take them in with you, then let them help you with little tasks at home that are similar to what you do at work. If you're a waitress pretend that the way they help you set the table is just like a real job. If you are an accountant teach them how to use Excel or let them staple something.

➡ **5.** Get them in on the act of becoming a SuperHero. Pick up a copy of the upcoming book "SuperHero Kids" and help them build an identity just like you did. Outward Bound offers adventures for kids as young as 12. Design a theme bedroom from Pottery Barn Kids. Exercise with them and praise them for their strength.

➡ LEARN A FOREIGN LANGUAGE

You will learn a foreign language to increase your mastery of communication. This will help you in any job you have. You will increase your overall skill level, you will be more qualified to travel abroad on company missions. In learning another language, you will have a greater understanding of the English language, as well as how language works in general. The number of people with whom you can establish a rapport will multiply. If you have mastered this power, you can also Teach English as a Foreign Language all over the world (tefl.com). Use this skill to see the world, if that's what you want. No matter what your goal or desire, there are always many routes. By learning a foreign language, you will gain flexibility in many areas of your life.

Use these five steps to begin your training:

➡ **1.** Consider which language would be most valuable for you to study based upon your own goals and mission requirements. Consider the language of a region you want to visit, or choose a commonly spoken language like French or Spanish.

➡ **2.** Take out language tapes from your local library or buy them from a bookstore.

➡ **3.** Establish your confidence in speaking by conversing with someone you know that speaks the language, if possible. You can also sign up for a class at a community college.

➡ **4.** Begin to get more comfortable with the language in the environments with which you are already comfortable: speak French with the owner at a French restaurant in your neighborhood. You will command respect from others in respecting their language.

➡ **5.** Immerse yourself in a place that primarily uses this language. You may not have to travel far. Remember, the United States has no national language. We are a nation of many cultures, languages and people. Reach out to new people with this ability.

➡ PUBLIC SPEAKING

This is a common fear. You must rise above this. Speak in front of people with the knowledge that you are a SuperHero, that the people who have come to listen, need to look up to you. Know that you give people hope, that you must live up to their expectations. Do not let this intimidate you, instead allow it to inspire you. You cannot fall prey to the thought of failure. You must succeed, knowing of your possibility for utter greatness. With strong oratory skills, you will immediately establish yourself as a powerful leader. Master this skill. Learn to speak with confidence, with ease and with eloquence. This power will carry you far, in your job, during your missions, and as a SuperHero.

Here are five points to quickly improve your SuperHero oratory skills:

➡ **1.** Hold your posture strong and project out from your diaphragm when you are speaking. Speak in a strong, unwavering voice. Never lose your posture. When others are watching you, you must project absolute confidence.

➡ **2.** Speak directly to the audience; always make solid eye contact. Make your eye contact so powerful that others avert their eyes.

➡ **3.** Use stories to personalize your speech and connect with your audience. Enchant and delight the people to whom you are speaking. Evoke emotion with your stories. Make them touching and purposeful.

➡ **4.** Hold your space, move around and use bold gestures. Remember: you are a SuperHero. This will enhance the showmanship, and maintain your look of confidence.

➡ **5.** Practice. Use a mirror, speak in front of friends, practice your commanding voice and presence everywhere you are. If this is a fear of yours, doing it often and in environments that are already comfortable for you will help you to become a superior orator.

➡ HUMAN LIE DETECTION

If you have studied your lessons well, you will understand that you posses this ability already. In studying, you will also have learned that there is much about an individual that is hidden to the untrained eye. There will be very little left hidden to you, however. You obviously know by now that a person's actions cannot easily be judged in a vacuum. You must see the larger picture. This power will help you with that.

These 5 steps must be your keys to unlocking the intentions of others.

➡ **1.** If you are an empowered, conscious being, the truth will be known to you already. This cannot be stressed enough. Don't "think" you know something. Simply know it. Trust your instincts.

➡ **2.** Watch the eyes of the person in question. Use the guiding phrase "Left: Lie / Right: Remember." If, as they face you, their eyes dart to your left, they are lying, creating, or imagining their story. If their eyes dart to your right, as they face you, they are remembering their story. In a small percentage of people this is reversed. Test your subject first with a question to which you already know the answer.

➡ **3.** Watch their breathing and heart rate. You do not need to touch them for this. Their heart rate will be known to you if you focus. Are they panicked? Does this increase at a particular point in the story?

➡ **4.** Watch their body for other clues. Are their pupils larger or smaller? Smaller may indicate a lie but must be corroborated with other signs. Watch for uncomfortable body language and tone. If they are uncomfortable, there is always a reason. Is their tone too aggressive? Too emotional? Or even too contrived? Watch carefully.

➡ **5.** Now you may gage their choice of words. This aspect is always last, always the least of your concern. You will know the truth before you reach this stage. Does the story include details about other people and their perception? When you delve into an area that is surprising, do they falter? Are the numbers and elements in the story too much in-sync?

➡ STEALTH

The power of stealth can come in handy on many occasions. It also has the unintended consequence of making one a better observer as well. The reason for this is simple: when in stealth-mode you are not there to act, you are there to blend. It forces you to use all of your abilities to accomplish this. That makes the power of stealth both offensive and defensive.

Here are the 5 keys to mastery of this power:

➡ **1.** Dial your energy way down. This is the most important step. Most often, when someone is caught, it is simply because their frequency was dialed up way too high. Think about this: have you ever passed by someone and just known that they were up to something? Try practicing on children, they are quite easy to read.

➡ **2.** Practice the second half of step one again. Learn to read when someone's energy is not right. It is always a dead giveaway.

➡ **3.** Never run when in stealth mode. If you are discovered there will be plenty of time to run then. This is about patience, conditioning, and proper use of your environment.

➡ **4.** Move as if you belong there. You can also be in stealth-mode while in public and indeed this is one of the best places to do so. Moving methodically also establishes authority, and most people have been trained to not ever question authority.

➡ **5.** Most often, you are the only one who knows your intentions. This means that you can calmly execute your plans by moving directly and calmly. Stealth can position you to be in the exact spot, every time. This isn't only about physical actions and plans, use this to maintain an air of stealth in all of your dealings.

THE POWERS OF THE FREE-RUNNER

Tactical Driving

Martial Arts

Small Arms Training

Knife Throwing

Lock-Picking

Survival Skills

Police Academy

Gadgetry

Parkour

➡ TACTICAL DRIVING

For the Free-Runner, this is an exciting choice for a power. It is also quite fun and will serve you both on, and off the job. It is, however, extremely dangerous. There are courses you can take that allow you to learn these skills safely. They are valuable skills to the SuperHero. Learn them, but do it safely, perhaps in an isolated area. As an aside, they may be rough on your vehicle as well.

With this in mind, here are 5 exciting techniques in summary from the websites Wikipedia, WikiHow, and a book called "Getaway," by George Eriksen.

➡ **1.** Know your car (and your equipment) as well as you know yourself: start small with swerves and emergency braking. Stay alert. Know the situation before there's a situation. Without having to check, you should know if there are cars around you or even in your blind-spot. Test yourself while driving: Without looking, what color is the car in your rearview mirror? How many passengers are in it?

➡ **2.** The Bootlegger's Turn instantly reverses the direction of your vehicle. Accelerate your vehicle to 40 mph. Pull the e-brake hard and sharply turn your steering wheel to the left about ¼ to ½ a turn. Your car should spin around and point in the opposite direction. Release the brake and get away fast.

➡ **3.** The Moonshiner's Turn will also reverse the direction of your vehicle, but is begun with the car absolutely still. Put the car in reverse and hit the gas. Count to five and then, all at once, hit the brakes (but don't lock them up!) and turn the wheel hard left. DO NOT HIT THE GAS. This must be all done simultaneously. When your car has spun around hit the gas and go. Fast.

➡ **4.** PIT Maneuvers in a car chase are straight-forward in nature. With the two cars rather side-by-side you align the front wheel of your car with the back wheel of their car. Because of the physics involved, the faster you are moving above 70 mph the more advantage you have and the less damage your car will suffer. At slower speeds you will have to hit their car harder. Simply tap the car you are pursuing by swerving into their back quarter panel. They spin, you win.

➡ **5.** Start slowly if you're using your own vehicle or perhaps take a professional course instead. It is great fun and very instructive.

➡ MARTIAL ARTS

The world of Martial Arts is indeed tremendous. There are many paths on which you may walk, and there are also many benefits. However, there are also pitfalls and even dangers along the way. All classes are not created equally, and not all will save your life. The skills you learn should not take you years, only weeks. Your choices here are critical.

We therefore can guide you with these 5 points of advice.

➡ **1.** Know your mission before you choose your art. Let it be said this way: be prepared most for the battle you will face next. Martial Arts in general are cooperative sports that are not aimed at saving your life. If you are the SuperHero type that will often be in physical danger, you will need something more appropriate. Perhaps combatives, or reality-based self-defense. My strongest recommendation for this type of mission: Krav Maga. Your prudent choices may save your life.

➡ **2.** Condition other areas of your fitness as well. To the SuperHero this is critical. Eat well and exercise. Get adequate sleep. Increase your cardio and stamina to incredible levels. To get winded or tired when you are facing a threat is foolish and suicidal. This is not the Way of the SuperHero.

➡ **3.** Find a training partner who is committed to your success. Meet with them. Workout with them. Grow and train with them. Push each other. Do not let the other person quit. Help them give their all, and they will do the same for you.

➡ **4.** Do not train only in the ways of your chosen discipline. This does not qualify as SuperHero training. Adapt what you have learned in your class to the mission you will face. The situational readiness you bring to the table will come from the martial base, but on its own, this base may not be enough.

➡ **5.** Meditate before and after training. It will keep things in perspective.

➡ SMALL ARMS TRAINING

Weapons are essential to the SuperHero. This is not meant to be pugilistic or war-mongering. Your greatest weapon is always your mind. Secondarily your body, and then only last comes any external device, however weapons are still key. And though this section focuses only on guns, do not come to over-rely on them. In fact, never do anything with a gun that you would not do without a gun. Most SuperHeroes do not use guns. A gun will make you weaker well before it ever makes you stronger.

Having said this, and understanding that the need may be great, here are 5 things to remember:

➡ **1.** Know your needs. If a gun is indeed your choice then spend time with professionals. Visit the local shooting range. Become a regular. Talk to the police in your area for proper licensing and permits. Do not talk to gun stores. Never take advice from someone who is trying to sell you something.

➡ **2.** Talk to the police. This is important and will hopefully keep you alive and out of custody. If you are hesitant to talk to the police about this, don't get a gun. It's that simple.

➡ **3.** Once you have your gun, focus *all* your training on using it for at least the first month. Afterwards, focus your next month of training as if you never owned one. A gun is not an ace-in-the-hole, nor a guaranteed win. In fact, you can bet on losing. By training diligently on using it, and then on not using it, you are prepared for both eventualities.

➡ **4.** Know when *not* to use a gun. There is an escalating scale and *this is in no way covered in this book*. If someone wants your money or property, give it to them. A gun is not a deterrent or a device to hold on to a few dollars. It is a device to save human lives.

➡ **5.** Only draw your weapon if you intend to use it. This is why you must train. Otherwise you risk it being used against you and those under your care. Do not use it as a way to scare someone.

➡ KNIFE THROWING

If you are indeed interested in weaponry of the conventional kind, you may find a course on knife throwing helpful. There are many ways. I will show you a few. This is to be used as a last resort. If you throw a knife at someone, you open the possibility for consequences you will have to live with for the rest of your life. As an aside, do you really want to basically toss your only weapon to a person who is threatening you? It's great in the movies but be sure this is what you want before you get yourself in a situation where it becomes your last mistake.

With due caution then, here are 5 pointers in successful knife throwing:

➡ **1. Extreme close range** means that you have no time for the knife to make any rotations (or flips) in the air (so why throw?). However, to do so, just open your hand, palm up, as if someone were putting money in it and lay the knife on top with the point already facing the target. Hold the knife with your thumb to keep it from falling. Swing your arm back, and using something like an underhand softball pitch, bring it forward again and release the knife in front of you when your arm is just a little below the target.

➡ **2. If you are about 10-15 feet away** the knife will make a half turn in the air when held with a "Horizontal Blade Grip." This looks like the hand gesture that Presidents use when speaking except this one has a knife in it. It is held by the entire blade (not just the tip) with the sharp edge away from your skin, with your thumb and forefinger as the primary gripping points. Bend your arm, and release the knife when your arm comes forward again. Do not flip it; release it straight. The knife will turn, point to the target, and stick hard, parallel to the ground.

➡ **3. Somewhere closer to 20 feet** the knife will need to make a full turn. Since a full turn means 360°, you must release it when it is already pointed towards the target. It will rotate all the way around again, and then stick. To do this, then, means you must hold it around the handle, like you would a hammer. This is an overhand throw. Again, you do not "flip" it. You release it straight-on by simply opening your hand when you are on target.

➡ **4. Beyond** this distance you will either need to increase the number of turns that your knife makes or, my personal favorite, just buy yourself a Flying Knife®. It will stick at any distance that you can hit with enough force. It is designed to always fly straight and never rotate. It's marvelous at its job and has stuck at distances of up to 60 feet. Even first time throwers can find success and never have to count turns. Again, it will stick at any distance.

➡ **5. Always make the same consistent movements.** Always. It is never a flipping motion, and you always throw with the same amount of force every time, no matter the distance. To increase number of rotations, grab less of the blade. To decrease rotations, grab more of the blade. Always throw the knife hard, especially if it's life or death. Just be prepared to live with your actions.

➡ LOCK-PICKING

Moving now to a skill that many in the criminal underworld already possess, we have the delicate art of lock-picking. This will take the diligent student near 5 minutes to learn and at most only a week to become proficient. The skills involved are simple, and the idea remains the same in all cases, only the finesse and feel will grow. Use this ability with caution and check with your local authorities to keep yourself from trouble. As always, train hard and constantly.

There are 5 areas of concern in your understanding of this endeavor.

➡ **1.** In the workings of a lock, you have a cylinder that is being kept from turning by way of metal pins standing in the middle of it. When using the proper key all of the pins are pushed into their proper locations and the cylinder will turn freely, thus, opening the lock. You will simulate this with your tools.

➡ **2.** By inserting a slim, pointed object (perhaps a modified safety pin), that has just the tip curved upwards slightly, you will find that you have access to these pins. It is a simple matter to use pliers to bend the tip. You will need one other tool for this: a tension wrench. This is a flat object that will turn the cylinder when the pins are in place.

➡ **3.** Practice first by poking and prodding the vertical, internal lock pins and watching them slide into place when pushed by your pick. They are not meant to slide all the way up. This will not open the lock. Even when you find the precise spot it will not open because they will keep springing back into place.

➡ **4.** To solve this, insert the tension wrench into the bottom of the lock key-way while you are manipulating the pins. Slightly turn the tension wrench as if it were an actual key, and keep gentle pressure on the tension wrench. Too much pressure will prevent it from opening. Both in concert will open the lock.

➡ **5.** Faster methods exist. Bump keys are simplistic, practically free to make, and can open any lock into which they fit. Any lock. The video is quite revealing.

➡ SURVIVAL SKILLS

You must learn to harness what you need when you find yourself without the luxuries of modern society. For if one day you find yourself ousted from your comfort zones, you will know how to re-build. For some, it may be knowing the plants that offer healing power or provide nourishment. For others, it will be bootstrapping a company together during an economic set-back. Understand how to satisfy your needs under any condition. Learn to make tools and weapons from the materials around you. Create. When you are in this situation, you will fully understand this. You will always be able to create anything when the need is present enough to you.

The topic of survival is very broad, so here are five points for you to begin your understanding:

➡ **1.** Consider your mission and the area you are in: what emergency situations might you encounter? Under what environments and conditions might you need to survive? Be ready for those. The others definitely won't happen, and even these may not.

➡ **2.** Prepare a survival kit relevant to your situation. It may include things like first aid, water purifying tablets, food procurement tools, shelter items, fire starting equipment in a waterproof case, or it may not. Terrain varies by hero. In the office, perhaps consider a portable set-up on a cell-phone that allows you to be completely mobile, yet efficient and sleek. Consider your terrain and plan accordingly.

➡ **3.** Learn how to identify and procure supplies to handle your mission, whether it is creating makeshift medical supplies or opening certain locks and defeating alarms. What would the elite of your profession carry?

➡ **4.** In the wild, learn how to build a shelter for yourself with the tools in your survival kit. In civilization learn how to build a financial shelter for yourself in times of economic need. Learn to read the conditions of the upcoming weather well—both natural and financial.

➡ **5.** In the wild, learn how to find different sources of water and learn the processes of purification. In the office, your life-blood is your people. Learn to find the people you need to have with you to accomplish your mission. Take note of their strengths, that they may be called upon in your times of need.

➡ POLICE ACADEMY

For the truly committed, enroll in a Police Academy class. The information you learn will be invaluable. The dedication you put forth by completing such a class will be evidenced in the skills you take away. Basic training covers driving skills, firearms, human relations, physical fitness, self-defense, and strategy & tactics. You do not have to become a police officer. Use this class to your full advantage. Take what knowledge you can from the instructors, master the skills. If you are committed to your mission, the hundreds of hours you put in here will aid your mission immensely. Use the class to establish your SuperHero network. Everyone in your class will not be a SuperHero or even interested in ascending, but it is a better pool of options. Be aware of those who stand out in your class. If you choose to make this investment, you will gain much from the experience.

Five steps to becoming a cadet:

➡ **1.** Begin a physical fitness program on your own (Chapter 10). If you are already in good physical condition, you will get more out of their fitness training.

➡ **2.** Research the basic academy class options in your area. Consider how it will fit into your schedule.

➡ **3.** Sign up for the class that you find will most meet your needs, and get family support... you may need it.

➡ **4.** Fully commit to the training, now that you have a better under-standing of the word. Study at home. Also: continue your own physical fitness routine.

➡ **5.** Ascend. Do what it takes to be the best, the strongest, the most powerful in your class. Consider this the first test of your ability to rise to answer your call.

➡ GADGETRY

Gadgetry is tricky since it may not even mean what you think it means. Gadgetry is about transforming the environment around you. It is finding use in objects you have, acquiring tools that will aid you further, and then also creating gadgets you need. It will allow you to become a master of your surroundings. Anyone can have this power, if they so choose. It is not just for engineers or technology buffs that own the latest toys on the market.

You can master the power of gadgetry by understanding the 5 following points:

➡ **1.** First consider your mission and the type of SuperHero you are becoming. What tools will you need? What everyday items will serve your purpose? What items are already on the market that you may use as SuperHero gadgets?

➡ **2.** Always think critically about everything that is around you. Mas-tering the core exercise of being able to re-create your environment with your eyes closed will aid you greatly here since your recall will tell you where to get what you need and how to use it.

➡ **3.** Think about how you can transform any object around you into a tool. Consider what you can use in your environment. Will you have to stab an enemy with a pencil, defend yourself with your keys, or pick a lock with a bobby pin? Find new uses for familiar objects, create new objects by combining different implements around you.

➡ **4.** Re-create (or at least stock) your familiar environments (such as your home or workplace) with the gadgets you have developed as well as the everyday objects that you will use. Make them accessible to you. This will be helpful in building a lair, but will also help you if should find an immediate need for them.

➡ **5.** Know how to think on your feet, how to be in the moment, and to consider how the things that surround you will provide all the help you need, in any situation. When you are not in your own familiar environ-ment, this will greatly serve your SuperHero quests.

➡ PARKOUR

This power will teach you to use your physical surroundings to your benefit. The world will literally become your playground; you will face no struggle in your physical endeavors. Parkour allows you to move with great speed and ease in any environment. You will instantly have an advantage over anyone that might chase you or attempt to fight you in your SuperHero quest. This sport not only develops your physical strength, but it also develops the ability of your mind. Research David Belle (Chapter 3). He has literally jumped from tall buildings with incredible flair and seeming ease. There is no obstacle that you cannot surmount in Parkour. When you know this is true in every situation, you will truly be on your way to becoming a SuperHero.

Use these 5 steps to begin:

➡ **1.** Find a qualified teacher. There are resources online and through Google.

➡ **2.** Begin training outside, not in the gym. This will help you gain real world skills quicker, and will ultimately protect you more as you gain respect for your art. The gym is padded. The real world is not. Train how you fight, for you will certainly fight how you trained.

➡ **3.** Practice often and with others. The synergy will do you good. Stretch. Do pull-ups. Strengthen your grip. Use a gymnastics class to help get limber.

➡ **4.** Respect the moves, the ground, your body, and your peers. It may sound obvious but this isn't about challenging others. It is about challenging yourself.

➡ **5.** Begin on low curbs. Jump back and forth between concrete parking blocks. It will help you begin to size up your abilities and your body in general. Climb trees and ropes. Increase your arm strength, but also your cardio capacity and your endurance.

THE POWERS OF THE FLYER

Remote Viewing

Lucid Dreaming

Out-of-Body Experiences

Precognition

Quantum Healing

Traditional Chinese Medicine

Shibumi

➡ REMOTE VIEWING

The power to see anything, regardless of its position in time or space is well within your reach. It is accessed by Remote Viewing and is one of the simplest powers you will learn. Once you are familiar with the basic concepts, the rest is simply application and practice; nothing more. When you remote view, you connect to the universal unconscious and document whatever you find about your target.

Here are 5 powerful keys to success:

➡ **1.** You begin with an ID number for a target. This tells your mind what the focus is to be. Depending on your goals for the exercise, you may or may not already know what the target is. These are two sets of four-digit numbers that are chosen at random to differentiate one target from another target. While training, have your partner place a magazine image in an envelope and write this ID number on the outside. The magazine image inside is what you will determine.

➡ **2.** Place your pen on the paper. When they read you the number you will notice an automatic flinch in your hand. All of the information about the target is contained in that flinch; all of it. This is why it is key to have your pen already on the paper. This transmission is key. Whatever initial movement your hand makes is exactly what gets transferred to the paper: just a quick flick of a pen-mark. This is your ideogram and will be probed for information. The beginning RV'er is usually taught to learn the first four ideograms of Water (wavy line: ~), Structure (90° angle: ⌐

or $\ulcorner$), Mountain (diagonal up, then diagonal down: ∧), and Land (flat line:—).

➡ **3.** Place your pen on the ideogram to begin decoding it. Go step by step asking about the motion you made, and the feeling it conveyed. For each question touch the ideogram and ask, then write down the answer. Maintain the structure of the questioning in order to keep the conscious mind busy. Write down all of your answers to these questions as well. Afterwards, move to these specific questions, in order: color, texture, smells, tastes, temperature, sounds, dimensions. Write down a list of one-word answers for each of these questions.

➡ **4.** After that phase, make a larger drawing of the ideogram by following the motions you listed in step 3 and then begin to probe it with questions as well.

➡ **5.** When you have come to the end of the probing questions, you are to put the pen down and make a determination on the content of the target. If any of these ideas come to you during the other phases immediately put down your pen and dismiss them as workings of the rational mind. It is only after you are done probing that your mind is allowed to extrapolate.

➡ LUCID DREAMING

As you have no doubt seen from the preceding power, the subconscious mind is extremely powerful. To tap into the incredible store of knowledge it offers has tremendous value for the SuperHero. Imagine being able to tap into any knowledge contained within and you will understand the value of this power.

Here are 5 key techniques in Lucid Dreaming:

➡ **1.** The way to trigger a lucid dream is to recognize that you are dreaming. If you come to this conclusion while in a dream you can wake up mentally, but remain asleep physically. Once completely conscious you will have absolute control over the elements in the dream realm. Colors will be more crisp and vibrant, sounds will have a crystal clarity. Indeed the world is already this way, it is only our choice of limits that keeps it hidden.

➡ **2.** There are several ways to become lucid: try to find your hand while in a dream. Once you have found it, by searching for it consciously, you will have become lucid. Another way is to always ask the question "Am I dreaming?" during your every day, waking life, eventually it will be asked automatically in your dreams as well. Yet another way is to notice continuity or logic errors in your dreams. Once you do you will understand that you must be dreaming.

➡ **3.** Once you have become lucid the excitement begins. You can visit any historic time and place while you are completely mentally awake. You can solve problems easier by integrating the two sides of your mind. You can overcome mental roadblocks and challenges that you suffered in your waking life. But probably the best fun of all is: you can totally fly! Try it... it's amazing. Begin by running and sort of, diving a little bit. Then move to some low-level flights, and then eventually take off and soar wherever you desire, with no limits.

➡ **4.** If you find that you are about to come out of your dream, or find that you are losing lucidity while in the dream, you can try a technique called dream-spinning. Once you know that you are losing the sight picture, simply have your dream persona spin around in tight circles recalling the exact name (and perhaps date) of this location. Just for clarity: you simply spin around and around in the dream with the intention of staying lucid. Do this and you will be able to explore much longer.

➡ **5.** This can be used as a tool to make clear and insightful decisions, to research data stored in your subconscious, to overcome fears, or even to set up a controlled environment in which to test a theory. It is a very powerful way to tap into the capabilities of the mind.

➡ OUT-OF-BODY EXPERIENCES (OBEs)

Being more than just your physical body opens up the door for exploration, and mapping out new territories of consciousness is definitely on the to-do list of the aspiring Flyer. The Flyer realizes that their mind is all-powerful, and as such, strives to gain an increasing amount of control over it. An out-of-body experience is one such way. People have reportedly used this technique to travel to distant lands and also to look in on close friends. Understanding your abilities is the first step to mastery. Separate yourself from your physical body and see where it will take you.

Here then are 5 steps that will guarantee you an OBE (with enough practice, that is):

➡ **1.** Reading books on the subject will send a signal to your unconscious mind, telling it that you really want this to happen. Especially if you read them right as you are falling asleep.

➡ **2.** Clearly saying to yourself as you fall asleep that you "will have an out-of-body experience tonight," and then allowing yourself to feel how good that will feel when you do have it. This part is crucial and works with everything from waking up without alarm clocks to having the car of your dreams. Act as if you already have it (or have experienced it) and really feel how good it feels to have it. Make sure your mind and body know how good it feels to receive these gifts. Then just let it go, and your subconscious will bring it about.

➡ **3.** Next, exploring the hypnagogic state is a more than just a good starting point, it's practically a launch-pad. When you are in that phase between being asleep and being awake, you are already 8/10 of the way there. Your goal while in this state is to simply disconnect from your body. Shut out the stimulus of the outside world completely and you will have done it. Detach from all external sounds and feels, and instead turn your attention inward. You must be absolutely physically relaxed to do this. Relax every part of you—completely. Then: become fully conscious inside your mind with no connection to, nor any stimulus from, the outside world.

➡ **4.** Once you have done this, you will have activated your astral body. Now that you have, there are many ways to disengage it from your physical body: rocking back and forth with increasing strength until you just "pop" right out; grabbing the rope that is hanging above your eyes and pulling yourself up, hand-over-hand; rolling over and out of the body; sitting up; seeing a spot in the room and getting up to walk over to it; And finally, easiest of all—just doing it.

➡ **5.** As one final piece of advice, you may find that you are less likely to fall asleep during practice if you attempt this when you have just woken up, rather than just gone to bed.

➡ PRECOGNITION

See the future. It is right before you. Every sign you need to see to tell you what people will do or say next is developing at this very moment. If you learn to pick up on the signs, or everything that is around you, you will know the future, at least the immediate future. With enough practice at reading the signs you will be able to expand this. You will find that you are able to respond before anyone else even knows what has happened.

➡ **1.** Be open to everything around you. Constantly take in every part of your surroundings that you can. The more with which you are familiar and the more to which you are attuned, the more things you will pick up.

➡ **2.** Pay close attention to body language and the specific words people are using in your conversations with them. These are two very strong indications of what they are thinking of feeling. Changes in body language and use of language will allow you to sense their changes in behavior as well.

➡ **3.** Trust your instincts. This is key to developing your power of pre-cognition. Different signs of body language, a different feel of energy in a place will offer you the knowledge of future happenings if you trust your instincts on what these changes mean. For example, if in a fight you keep contact with a person as they fall to the ground, you will be able to know instantly when their direction and intention changes because their muscles tense as a precursor to an attack.

➡ **4.** Abandon your preconceived notions. Just because you think something will happen a certain way does not mean that it will. Staying open to everything that is going on around you will be a much better indicator of the future.

➡ **5.** Gradually increase the area of which you can be completely aware. You may take this to mean time or space. The greater area of which you are aware, the larger the shifts you will notice, and therefore the greater magnitude of events you will foresee as a consequence. Now decide how you will use this power.

➡ QUANTUM HEALING

The mind is powerfully connected to the body, especially when it comes to the ability of the body to heal. It is not necessary to prove this to you, because it is true. In healing another, you must first understand that it is not you that does the healing; only that you assist them in healing themselves. You are more like a guide in the process. This power will strengthen your own mental strength as well. Use the resources provided for you to learn more about this, however you may also begin with these 5 steps.

➡ **1.** Focus on your breathing. Take deep, powerful breaths. Take a quick breath in for two seconds and then breathe out slowly for four seconds. Use your breath to gather the energy in your body. Breathing is key to this power.

➡ **2.** Know your intention. It is not to heal, but to reach the other person's mind, so that they may heal their own body. You must create the most powerful and positive energy within you that you can in order to do this.

➡ **3.** Know the outcome. Know with all of you that this will aid the person in need, that they will be able to heal themselves with your help.

➡ **4.** Place your two hands around the body part in need of healing. Focus on the energy that has built up inside of you.

➡ **5.** Continue to maintain the deep breathing, maintain your high level of positive energy flow to the person in need. You are attempting to reach their mind, to transform the low energy they have in their body. Hold your intentions and you will soon see your ability to aid another.

➡ TRADITIONAL CHINESE MEDICINE (TCM)

The scope of healing practices in this area is wide, and there is much to study and learn. Study will indeed serve you well. Eastern medicine practices revolve around the idea that the body is a complete universe. This point you must stop and fully understand. You are a complete universe. TCM relies upon the concept of Chi or Qi, which is the life flow of energy through the body. It works to balance and restore the body's Chi.

Read about the following 5 points of TCM. Decide what will aid you and delve in deeper. This field is a source of much power:

➡ **1.** Acupuncture relies on the foundation that the body is made up of different acu-points that may be stimulated by needles to correct disruptions of bad energy flow. Bad energy flow is the cause of emotional and physical health problems in a person.

➡ **2.** Acupressure relies on these same acu-points as a guide to a person's body. Instead of a needle, pressure is applied to these points with the hand or elbow, for example. Fire cupping is a variation on acupressure.

➡ **3.** Qi-gong translates to energy work. This relies on the use of breathing and movement exercises which is used to maintain health and also in used Chinese martial arts.

➡ **4.** Tui Na is a form of manipulation therapy through the use of therapeutic massage. Therapeutic moves include pushing, pulling and pinching the skin in order to correct energy imbalances.

➡ **5.** Learn a technique, study one in depth. When you have the ability to help correct another's energy (with their cooperation), you will have great powers to heal and restore the energy of another's life. Just as you can use this power to help someone, you can also use this in combat.

➡ SHIBUMI

How does one describe effortless perfection? Indeed Trevanian has done so in his novel of the same name (Shibumi. Ballantine. 1979), but how does this translate to the SuperHero and how easy is it to teach? What does it mean to showcase "being, without the angst of becoming?" It is clearly too great a concept for words. In the Tao Te Ching we are taught that "The Way that can be described is not the true Way." I will therefore offer you indicators to be cultivated, more than steps to becoming. Please accept my paraphrasing of the original as an attempt to elucidate a vague understanding. This describes an amazing essence... I wish you the best.

Here are 5 milestones on the path to Shibumi:

➡ **1.** There is a natural flow to the Universe. If one were to describe it as a stream, those who are not in the flow are spinning aimlessly in an eddy off to the side. Those who are in the flow have shot immediately forward and are carried effortlessly along the path. They are in, on, and of, the stream. It is the effortless moving through life, as if always in a smooth glide, with illusions falling to either side of you.

➡ **2.** In manifestation, it would be likened to hurtling down the freeway, witnessing all sorts of cars crashing in front of you, and simply sidestepping them all with a smooth, easy motion... because in that perfection, at that exact moment, with all sound completely stopped... it is only your effortless precision from one movement to the next that matters or even remains.

➡ **3.** In appearance, it would be to possess a complete, yet light, smile that appears because there is no longer anything else to overcome. Simply because nothing else can even exist... nothing except being... and so you simply are... and you are eloquently silent.

➡ **4.** In learning, it would be complete understanding, rather than full knowledge... because understanding permeates all things, while simple knowledge can only specify.

➡ **5.** It is to walk in a pure Truth and to know that you are the absolute authority of your own Creation. You possess the indomitable ability to write your own Destiny. You are the Omniscient Bodhisattva and the Omnipotent Creator. You are the Power and the Light, and in the totality of your life, as with all of the things you do... this is simply being... and you simply are.

For you are a SuperHero... and you are ready.

The Mind Leading the Blind

A FIRST LOOK AT FINDING PROFESSOR X

A First Look at Finding Professor X

In following all of the steps, you now know that you are at your peak physically. You will have gained amazing insight, memory, and skill. You are qualified, even as we speak to begin any number of careers that were previously closed to you. Your Core powers alone are enough to place you head and shoulders above the rest. I applaud you. More so: I respect you.

In this chapter, as in all the others, you must continue your growth. What powers you have found appropriate, you must now train. You can not afford to pretend you know them from only a minute's reading. You must now take up a course of study in your specific powers. This is where you specialize, and as such I will suggest places for you to do so.

All SuperHeroes have the core. Basic training is only that: basic. Now you need your own, unique path. This is where the mentor comes in.

In the comic book world, Professor Charles Xavier, of the Xavier institute, was an amazing mentor. Indeed Professor X, the consummate professional, taught his students everything from combat to philosophy. He trained many a SuperHero in his day, and it was not uncommon for him to be sought out because of this. He was so influential and well-known in fact, that his pupils often became better known by using a part of his name, rather than their own. Hence: The X-men.

Your Professor X, your mentor, can guide you in the same way; just as the comic book version has done for his students. You can learn to develop not only your SuperHero powers, but also the other areas of your life as well.This chapter will act as a guide to help you find this person. Begin to consider: what goals do you have for a mentor? What can they teach you? What aspect of your SuperHero identity can a mentor help to develop more fully?

All of these questions of course presuppose that you can even find one. Further, that you can find one who understands the world of the SuperHero. Well, as ~~luck~~ preparation would have it, you can always find one using the resources below. But then, you knew I was going to say that, didn't you?

COMMUNITY COLLEGE COURSES

Enrolling in community college courses is a great way to find your Professor X, as well as to develop your powers, and I like this one a lot. This path also has the advantage of being incredibly inexpensive and accessible to everyone. Classes are usually about $20 a unit and begin every few months. Since many community colleges accommodate students going back to school, there are usually choices of night classes and even weekend classes that can fit into the schedule of any budding SuperHero. Schools are open to everyone, regardless of former education and the class list can be amazing.

What's most important is understanding how to use what may seem like a regular class, in ways that only a SuperHero would. For example, yes, Batman studied chemistry, just as thousands of people have, but very few have ever applied the learning in the way he did. What would a SuperHero do with a welding class? Micro-Electronics? Surfing? Get the picture?

Taking a class with a goal in mind is always a powerful choice. This does not have to be degree-oriented (although there's nothing wrong with an educated SuperHero), nor does it have to be a full-time commitment. Simply committing yourself to taking one class every semester can be very helpful to becoming a SuperHero. The skills you can learn are unending!

If this is the route you will take perhaps some pointers are in order.

➡ START BY LINING UP YOUR SUPER-POWERS.

As always, the best way to get somewhere is to know where you are going. By first imagining your ideal SuperHero self, and then forming a list of your desired super-powers, you can structure your community college classes accordingly. Take those that will further your mission and your goals. Stay away from those that have been some life-long curiosity. This is about focused results, not scratching some 10-year long itch. Once you are finished with your SuperHero training, you can always go back and learn more.

➡ CHOOSE CLASS TIMES THAT FIT WITH YOUR LIFE.

If going to class isn't a natural extension of what you do now, you my just end up skipping them. Bad idea. To avoid this, choose times that actually work for you and take into account the other elements of your life as well. Get a study partner if that helps.

➡ CHOOSE A PROFESSOR WITH POTENTIAL.

The best professors are the ones that make themselves accessible to their students. Most teachers love to help dedicated students, especially when students are enthralled with the material they teach (which you will be, since you have only chosen classes that revolve around your new identity).

With your new powers to understand and read people, you will be able to identify this type of teacher on the first day of class. Ask the professor when "office hours" are. When you do, watch for body language and tone... this will help you discern how committed they are to their students. You can also tell by simply watching how they are with other students. Do they seem interested? Are they only there to punch a clock and head home?

Remember, you are searching for a mentor, choose carefully. Everywhere you go, there are people that are SuperHeroes and people that simply are not. As an aside, they don't have to agree to mentor you for them to be effective. Take the class that furthers your goals. Don't forget why you're here.

➡ FOCUS AND COMMIT.

When you have found an interesting class and an excited professor, take advantage of this! You're paying for it, after all. Get the most out of it you can. Be enthusiastic; participate! Apply your SuperHero self and master the material. Chat with your professor after class. Go to office hours. You did ask when they were on the first day of class, after all!

Quality teachers love to help. Talk to them about your goals, about what you want to achieve. The professor is a master of the subject they teach. If a strong rapport is established, he or she may be interested in becoming your mentor himself. At the very least, your professor can point you to other valuable resources, and perhaps refer you to a colleague that may be more knowledgeable on your particular area of interest.

➡ EXPLORE.

Any type of SuperHero can benefit from instruction at a community college. If you are a Freelancer, consider learning a computer program or taking a management course that might help you move up in your job. Consider also learning a new job to expand your skill set. (See the section below on vocational schools.) If you are a Free-Runner, consider the track team, surfing, or rock climbing.

You can also take a class on something that will add to your training regimen you might not have previously considered. Consider a dance class, a Yoga class or a weight training class, perhaps. If you are a Flyer, dive into a subject completely outside of your realm of knowledge. It might sound like common sense, but simply learning something new expands your mind. Consider quantum physics or even massage, for example. See no limits to how you can use this opportunity!

SPECIALIZED CLASSES AND SCHOOLS

Vocational schools or programs that offer very specific courses of study are another means to develop your powers. This is a very good plan of action for the SuperHero in training that knows exactly what they would like to learn. It is also usually for someone who has more time to dedicate to their training. Consider aviation school, robotics, or criminal justice, for example. Also, the teachers will have a more in-depth base of knowledge and may thus make for more accessible and specific mentors.

Even though these programs are very specific, there is still an unending amount of things you can do with the knowledge.

This path will take more commitment then just taking one course. Trade, or vocational schools often require full-time enrollment. However they still cater to people going back to school and non-traditional students, and will often offer a course of study at night or on the weekends. If this sounds appealing, start looking at what vocational schools are in your area and when you can enroll. You should also still investigate the local colleges in your area to see if you can take specialized classes for what you want to learn. Often, attending a full-time program is not your only option.

MENTORSHIPS

There are many different places you can go to find a mentor. If you are a former college student, visit the alumni association of your school. The alumni is made up of people that are now well-established and who have a passion for the school. It follows then, that they are usually very excited to guide a fellow person of their alma mater. Make connections with them and they will be happy to lend you their own resources. Find out what their path was to get where they are today. This can be a powerful source of information and guidance.

Work places often have mentorships available as well. In fact, a mentor is usually thought of in terms of a person's career. Talk to your boss to see if the company you work for now has any type of mentorship program. If business is your thing, SCORE offers free counseling to small businesses, and you can even pick a person. Even if your SuperHero mission and identity are beyond the scope of any one, particular job, there might still be people that use the powers you would like to master within their jobs. Find the overlap.

If these options don't fit your needs, be proactive about finding yourself a mentor on your own. Do your research. Contact top professionals in the industry that can help you. Contact people who are active in the field or area that you want to learn. Use the Internet. Anybody can be successfully reached these days.

Many will be flattered that you would like them to mentor you. Some however, will just be sign posts to help you find other resources, or they may be too busy to help you themselves. The most important thing here is knowing what you want from the mentorship, what you want to learn and what your goals are. Look to the mission and vision statements that you have already written. Who can you contact that will be an ideal resource to help you reach the image you are creating?

THE MORPHEUS INSIDE YOUR HEAD

It is also quite possible you may not even need a mentor. In fact, you may be the best person qualified for this job. Try this: Stop everything for a moment. Stay still and quiet. There is a voice inside of you, inside everyone. Sometimes we are too busy distracting ourselves with what we think we should be doing, or with what other people are telling us to do, to listen to it. When you do listen to it... things get done. Things become real. When you listen, what do you hear? What do you want more than anything? If you have never heard this voice before, what would it say to you if you could hear it? If you are a quote person, I saw one on a coffee cup that may fit: "What would you attempt to do if you knew you could not fail?"

" True understanding lies within. Find your own Professor X in the folds of your being.

Maybe even watching TV is the right answer. The show America's Next Top Model, for example is one of the best examples of a mentorship on television today. Far better than The Apprentice, for my money. Let me explain.

If you watch her show (Tyra Banks), you are shown exactly what to do to become not just an average model, but a damn good model. If someone were to watch every episode of that show from beginning to end, and actually apply the advice they give, that person would be quite near unstoppable in that industry. For all intents and purposes, Tyra Banks then, is a great SuperHero mentor... if your goal is to become a fashion model, that is.

She can teach success because she herself has succeeded. But here's what's so great about it: you don't even need to be a contestant. Just watch the show and pay attention to all the free advice (you can skip all the caddy interactions between the contestants). Compile it the right way, and Tyra is your new secret weapon.

So why is Tyra Banks in the section about teaching yourself? It's simple, really. By watching a DVD of the show, or even seeing them when they first air, you are really teaching yourself. It isn't her, as much as it is your desire to learn it and to be taught. Granted she laid the groundwork, but now the real effort has to come from you. If being a model isn't your thing, then watch the show Plain Jane. She has normal girls jump out of planes and stand in shark tanks; but at the end of the day they face their fears, get the guy, and grow tremendously on the inside. And if you watch her, you will learn. In baseball it would be like watching the pitcher while he is pitching and then pretending that you, yourself, are pitching while checking yourself in the mirror in order to practice your form. My dad did that. He now does everything with his right hand except throw, because he taught himself in the mirror. Here's another example: When I was in the Navy there was a guy who didn't know how to swim that wanted to be a Navy SEAL so badly, that he actually practiced swimming across the floor the entire night before his test. The next day, he passed with flying colors.

In the end, the path doesn't matter. When you are truly committed to a goal, the path will appear before you, it will forge itself. The mentor is only an illusion. It is always you that remains, that endures. It is always your choice to succeed. When you really listen to this voice, when you start taking steps toward what you want, you will have it. It will be yours sooner than you can imagine.

In <u>The Matrix</u>, Morpheus guides Neo to becoming the One, but it is only when Neo understands things on his own that he indeed becomes it. He simply is, rather than just being guided or taught. The true understanding lies within. Find your own Professor X in the folds of your being. Bring them back from banishment and they will reward you with everything you can imagine.

➨ THE GUARANTEED APPEARANCE

There is a reason this section appears here, at the end of all the other methods. It is here because if you have been doing each step as they have been presented, you will be in the exact place you need to be in order to find your mentor. You may have heard this concept referred to in many ways throughout your life.

In a movie it was said "if you build it, they will come." The Buddhist proverb puts it more like "when the student is ready, the master will appear." In business you may have heard that "the person who gets promoted to a position is the one who is already doing the job and just not being paid for it." These are all true, and they speak to one, central fact: Commitment.

When you commit to doing something, in the ways previously discussed, you will find that the universe realigns itself to bring about the things you need. Consequently, your belief in this concept isn't necessary—it just happens. What this means is that if you want to find a mentor, start doing what it is you want to learn, start being who you want to be. That person will show. Statement of fact.

Said differently: If you do everything you can to immerse yourself in what you wish to learn, and in what you want to be, you will definitely become what you want. You will, because you are already doing it in every way that you can. This really emphasizes the concept of commitment.

You already have a mythology, a mission statement, and you may even have begun to develop your powers. Decide what you want, do it with focus and you will not only find a mentor, you will become the very thing you have designed. In fact, a mentor may actually seek you out as a way to accomplish his or her own ends (perhaps finding an heir to which they can pass information, or perhaps to complete a mission).

None of these steps are very hard. It is quite easy to take a class, to contact a professional in a field you want to understand and even to listen to what is already inside of you. It is, however, the complete commitment that often becomes difficult for people. But if your desire is strong, if you know what you want, even commitment will not be hard. It is simply going after the very thing you want to become; it is creating yourself in the very best way you can. Consider the Buddhist proverb and be ready. This is the most direct path to finding your Professor X.

Power-Tools

FIRST LOOK AT WIZARD WANDS, UTILITY BELTS, MAGIC LASSOS

A First Look at Wizard Wands, Utility Belts, Magic Lassos

Show of hands: How many of you have been waiting for this chapter, crazily anticipating all the power you will wield once your arsenal is complete? Hmm. I thought so.

For the most part, your tools will be specific to the powers and skill-set you have chosen. For example, a lawyer and a police officer may both fight crime, but just try arresting a criminal with a legal brief and watch what happens! Because they are specific to your trade, you will most likely have them given to you (or suggested to you) by your master, mentor or professor. They know what challenges others in your chosen field have had to face, and can make recommendations to you to help you become more successful than your predecessors. However, this chapter would be really boring if that was all I said, so perhaps I should offer you a few starter points (and at least a few places to find tools); especially considering the length of time we have spent together.

As we have seen, SuperHeroes come across many different circumstances in their daily lives, and the tools they choose will often decide how they handle things. After all, if all you have is a hammer, you will treat every problem like a nail. You'll also notice that SuperHeroes, by-and-large, usually seem to get the job done with a minimum of wasted effort. This means their selection has been well thought-out for the challenges they are most likely to face, but because of all this, there is a large catalog of SuperHero items in circulation today.

With so many items to cover, and so many lines of work available to SuperHeroes today, it just isn't practical to go into every sort of power-tool available. These things being as they are, look at this chapter more as just an overview to help guide you to making your own choices, and not as an exhaustive list. Having said that, let's start with something fun.

HOW TO BUILD THE BATMOBILE

In the book <u>Rolling Thunder</u> (Kephart. Paladin. 1992) the prospective SuperHero can learn all about creating a car that is totally tricked-out, very much like the fabled Batmobile. It will tell you all about things like deploying defensive oil slicks to thwart whomever is chasing you, for example, or putting machine gun turrets in your grill, or maybe even adding some blinding beams of car-mounted light for stopping foes dead in their tracks. For the purposes of making weapons for your car... <u>Rolling Thunder</u> is absolutely great. It will tell you all that, and much, much more.

What it can't tell you however is how to make the actual Batmobile. Or even the reason

why the Batmobile is so amazing anyway. What I am getting at here is the difference between just adding things (or even buying them), solely for the sake of having them, as opposed to actually looking for the things you really need; the things that really are important to completing *your* mission.

You see, all the gadgets that Batman had were always great (the Batmobile included), because they were always exactly what was needed at the exact moment required to save Batman's life or to help him complete his mission. You can't buy that kind of preparedness at the Humvee store. Now don't get me wrong, it's not like a Humvee isn't an amazing piece of machinery if you are storming through the desert, but if you're just shopping at the mall then maybe it is just a little out of place.

The point I am making here is that your version of the Batmobile should suit you... not someone else. Consequently, you would equip it with all the things you need for your adventures and not theirs. For example, I have a friend who keeps a portable refrigerator in her car. To her kids, that's the right piece of equipment, at the right time, for their hot summertime travels.

To be completely obvious about it, if you are trekking through the jungle in search of a lost culture, then obviously the tools you need will be different than what you would need if you were carrying food to the homeless people downtown. In fact, if your mission *were* to bring food to the homeless, then you may just want to borrow my friend's electric refrigerator! Either way, both tasks are very heroic (finding lost civilizations and feeding the hungry and homeless), yet both are very different. Your Batmobile should be prepared to handle the environments that you are most likely to face, not someone else.

Allow me to make another key point here however. I already know that most of you who read this will just be commuting to work and back. Now I'm not saying you should only have the things needed for your commute in your car... I am saying that if you're going to be a SuperHero then you need to think (and act) like one. But as clear as that is, how does it fit into the question of your car?

Well, for starters: Don't carry just your suitcase, or your toolbox, or your schoolbooks... Bring things you can use for fighting crime (if that's your mission). Bring stuff for performing battle surgery or triage if that's your thing... Bring a store of well-rounded, easily dispensable food, or maybe a few children's toys—whatever it is, be prepared. And get your car into the act as well.

By the way, you may as well have your car at the ready because, as Americans, we spend on average an hour and a half in our car every day. That adds up to about 33 days a year! Imagine being able to spend that time living out your life's greatest SuperHero mission.

Now, let's go back to that <u>Rolling Thunder</u> book for a second, so I can mention some crossover items here that may work for everybody. For example, do you remember that blinding ray of light that I listed earlier? Well it can illuminate more than just crime. If your task is rescuing trapped hikers you might use it to find them, or to show them the way out. If it's feeding people on winter nights you can use the beam to set up your staging area. If it's lighting up a little league game, well obviously you're already prepared. Just figure out what you need and bring it along for the ride. Simple.

There are of course the other, more Batmobile like, things that you can add, and yes, the book does go over some of those things as well. For example, putting machine guns in the grill of your car is totally possible. Though this may make you less of a SuperHero, and more of a Super-Felon. How about adding those oil slicks, to better help you evade your pursuers? Or maybe you want to use some of those tire-spikes to pop their tires? Well just search the Internet, they're called caltrops and they're only $5.00. But I think that by now you probably get the picture. So let's move on, shall we?

A FEW SOURCES

Here are a few sources to help get you going in the right direction. As I mentioned, it isn't an exhaustive list. My only goal here was to provide you a little value for your money and get your own ideas cooking on the subject, and hopefully I have done that.

The first one probably falls under the category of "little-boy fantasy," but then, what of this book doesn't? They are the Punisher Armory books (part of the Punisher comic book series) and, yes, though it may be a little boyish, I practically drooled over these as a kid. I remember thinking about all the cool repelling gear I was going to buy so that I could escape down the side of a building in Manhattan. "Escape from whom?" certainly comes to mind. As does the fact that I have never actually been to Manhattan. But that never stopped me from dreaming about it.

On a more grown-up level, the Eastbay catalog is amazing. They have stuff in there that can actually add almost a foot to your vertical leap (helpful for Parkour if you chose that power in Chapter 12). In their catalog they also showcase a great line of clothing from the company UnderArmor (which is just plain cool) and shoes made from a fabric that is actually stronger than Kevlar! I better slow down here or that drool might come back.

You know, during the time I have been researching this book, it's starting to seem to me like the lost art of catalog shopping isn't half bad, and could in fact offer up a lot of choices: Kiefer, US Cavalry, Paladin Press, and High Voltage Press, for example. Online you can also find TheCoolHunter.net, ThinkGeek.com, and maybe even Dynamism.com. If this doesn't keep you busy for hours, you just weren't looking at it all.

Certain SuperHero types may also want to look at military surplus stores, security stores, and especially spy shops. Spy shops have way more stuff than you might ever use on a mission, but it is great to know it is all there if you ever need it. Other SuperHero types may even find it useful to have access to free books and information whenever they need them. Try Gutenberg, ManyBooks.net, the CIA World Factbook, The Action Hero's Handbook,

Google Earth or even Google Book Search... you may just be surprised.

These books aren't just about stopping bad guys either, and you may have noticed some of that above. For example if selling is your business, and you want to be a SuperHero of the Freelancer variety, head on over to TimeLineSelling.com. The secrets you will learn there are truly amazing, and, having seen them myself, I can certainly vouch for their effectiveness. You may also want to look up Mark Joyner for a few mental tips, tricks and resources to sharpen up your abilities as well. The possibilities are really endless.

The RLSHs have a guy named The Eye, who seems to make weapons for SuperHeroes, and you can also find other sources for tools and weapons online if that's your thing. But if you do, may I please suggest that you search for non-lethal weapons, or even EMD weapons? Just go with me on this one, it isn't really good form to run around killing everyone. Oh, their website also has a link for a place called Hero-gear. They offer some clothing and supplies, and it seems really cool (all the designs and such), though I can't vouch for them yet. Much of the same can be had at Eastbay, as well (and I can vouch for them)... but it may just not be so colorfully designed.

One final note... SuperHero groups seem to be springing up everywhere (they're just not all very serious about it yet). This may mean that you can link up with them for clothing, gear, or support. But again: I don't know them yet... therefore I am not recommending them, I can only suggest. Either way, I wish you great luck.

The best places to look, of course, are to the same places your mentors would go if they needed something in your field. I know that this list has offered a lot of things, from just a few types of missions, but this doesn't mean that the other requirements are out of luck—just that they have to be more creative for the same resources. Good luck, young Jedi.

THE SHOPPING LIST

And now for the place where the rubber meets the road and the credit card hits the counter. Buying toys for yourself is probably the most fun a person can have while shopping, and in fact, this was probably the most fun research project I did for the entire book! Unless I miss my guess, you will find this exercise to be great fun as well. This is where you get to create a shopping list of all the really cool things you think you need to become a full-fledged SuperHero. I loved it, and I don't even like shopping. The key thing you will notice here is just how tangible this goal really is. Once you see that the sum total of everything you want/need is only $1700 dollars (in my case, anyway), well... the rest just falls into place.

It is easier to just show you than it is to tell you, so here goes. You can work out the rest on your own. Just a note... it wasn't the research that was so fun... it was the dreaming of what can be and then finding out that things weren't as difficult as I would've imagined.

EXAMPLE FREE-RUNNER SHOPPING LIST

PD105 Dazzler (found one place ≈ 299)

Dyneema Vest IIIA (about $600)

M18L Taser (about $600)

Gun shaped OC Spray ($69)

Spy Glasses ($10 – why not?)

Pepper-Spray Ring ($30)

Maybe a telescoping stun baton ($60)

Hinge Cuffs (I own)

Nomex Body Suit (maybe $50 on e-bay)

Black body suit ($100)

Parkour Shoes ($ 89.99)

Memphis 9378T Kevlar Knit Sleeve ($4)

Honey-Grip® 9370H Coated Kevlar® Gloves ($53 by the dozen)

Anti-OC Gloss as a coating

EXAMPLE FREELANCER SHOPPING LIST

Amazon's Kindle (and a Library Card)

Mac Book Pro

Red Bull

IronKey Thumb drive (encrypts data)

USB Security Lock

TeleSpy Intrusion Detector

Hidden Wall Safe

Rubik's Cube

Spazzstick caffeinated lip balm

Asics' Eagle Trail Running Shoes

Nike Women's Pro fitted tops (various)

Nike Women's Personal Best Racing Shorts

Nike Women's Race Day Tech Tight

Pimsleur Language CDs (French, Spanish)

Emergency Phone Charger

Mindscape Brain Trainer

EXAMPLE FLYER SHOPPING LIST

Meditation for Beginners DVD ($11.98)

Technical Remote Viewing QuickStart System ($9.99 @ MatrixAccess.com)

The Brain Supercharger – Mind Lab ($199.95)

Advanced Ultra Meditation Mind-Tek Research ($49.95)

Zener ESP Testing Cards, $12.99 @ Amazon.com

Ok. Shopping's over. Hope you found some really cool stuff for yourself. Here's a self-test question: Did you think up what your missions would actually be like, before you made the list? Well... not to worry. In the next section we cover some of the greatest gadgeteers that have come before you. Let's see how they did.

THE GOLD STANDARD

Now... I know you know this one, but I still want to ask: Who has the greatest utility belt of all time? Yeah, you're right... that one was easy. Why it's Batman of course! Now, he may not have been the greatest gadgeteer of all time. I am sure some would say Iron Man, or heck, maybe even MacGyver. Ah, but for utility belts the gold standard has always been Batman.

On any given day the famous Bat Utility Belt might hold anything from a transistor radio built into the buckle to various tubes and devices ready to get him out of danger the very minute he needs it. Here is a random sampling from <u>Tales of the Dark Knight</u> (Vaz. DC Comics, Inc. 1989).

BATMAN'S UTILITY BELT	
Skeleton Keys & Lock Picks	Batrope
Rebreather	Laser Torch
Miniature Camera	Acids, Chemicals
Infra-red Flashlight & Lenses	Smoke Capsules
First Aid	Tear Gas Pellets
	Batarang

Of course this sort of preparation has it advantages, and it showed whenever Batman found himself in trouble. Maybe some of these items will work for you as well, maybe they won't, but like Batman, you'll want to make sure that even just using all these things isn't all you are able to do. You see, Batman had the ability to use his environment, and all the items within it, to overcome great obstacles as well. For example, in the book I just mentioned, he used a rusty cotter pin found on the ground to pick a lock, a wheelchair to break open a glass tank, and he broke a steam pipe to melt an ice prison he was in, while at the same time fogging up the room to conceal his actions.

But considering this is a section on all sorts of power tools, and not just utility belts, let's take a minute and cover the other two famous gadgeteers I mentioned above: MacGyver and Iron Man, and see where they fit in the scheme of things.

GADGETEERS GALORE

These two (MacGyver and Iron Man) run a bit of a parallel race in my view. In fact I see them as so close together, that I find it difficult to determine a true winner in the contest of Best Gadgeteer. What is so interesting to me about it all however, is not how closely they vie for 1st and 2nd, but how differently they both go about their tasks and challenges, and yet both find ways to always succeed. This reemphasizes the point in Chapter 10 (SuperHero Boot Camp) that your workout routine does not matter—it is only your commitment to the outcome that matters.

To begin with an overview of the two, MacGyver is a strong contender for top gadgeteer because of the way he handles his challenges. To the untrained eye, when MacGyver heads out to tackle a problem, he seems to go out unprepared, but this is not accurate. Not carrying every tool known to man, is not the same thing as being unprepared. No, when MacGyver heads out, he always brings with him the two most important tools he has (and I am not talking about a Swiss Army knife and duct tape either). MacGyver brings his mind and his training to bear on any challenge he has to face. Anything else he picks up along the way is just a means to an end. It seems that no matter what the challenge, MacGyver is always ready. Here are just some of the situations MacGyver has faced.

CHALLENGE	IMPLEMENT/SOLUTION
Diffuse Nuclear Warhead	Paper Clip
Sulfuric Acid Leak	Chocolate
Create Explosion	Cold Medicine
Deadly Laser Grid	Pack of Cigarettes
Transmit Morse Code	Light Switch

Now conversely we have, at the far end of the spectrum, Iron Man. I say far end because of the level at which Tony Stark (the man inside the Iron Man) creates his gadgets. Stark is an engineering wunderkind, accepted to MIT at 15 and graduated thereafter at the top of his class. As such, his level of gadgetry is often supremely amazing. Take for example his anti-gravity devices, or his various propulsion devices, hovercrafts, submarines, or jets

This of course says nothing about his amazing armor and its great capabilities, or even the specially-modified shield that he created for Captain America.

I would say that falling somewhere in the middle we find Batman in this world of gadgeteers, since his designs will usually fall somewhere in between those two people in terms of complexity and components used. As mentioned above, he has been known to use many common objects in a pinch (similar to MacGyver) but also has become fantastically well-known for his use of the high-tech gadgets (a la Tony Stark) that he creates in his laboratories as well.

The focus here though, as always, is not what they got out of it. It's what you get out of it. Lots of people want to wait until they have some great item, or perfect plan, or even a gym membership, before they go out and do battle with whatever particular oppression weighs them down. Learn from the successful. Go out now and use what you have to the best of your ability. The steps themselves are often enough to propel you to victory.

Building your Secret Lair

A FIRST LOOK AT THE HOUSE OF THE FUTURE

A First Look at the House of the Future

This chapter is all about creating the perfect space in which you will reside. It is about creating your home to reflect your new SuperHero identity. Not only is this an important step in cementing your new identity, but it also comes with lots of enjoyable activities. The image you have of your home (and your related associations therein) can be anything you like with just a few changes. Why not make it the best it can be?

SECRET ENTRANCE

Well if you haven't guessed, this section really isn't as much about re-building your front door (or installing a secret bookshelf with a two-way entrance) as much as it is about some special configuration to let you clearly know that you are now in SuperHero mode. Whatever it is that you use as a mental trigger it should, in the words of Joseph Campbell, signal your entrance into the special world. And this is really cool because it means that now you can have all sorts of special rules and behaviors that are starkly different from your normal world.

Many, if not all, SuperHeroes use this feature every day. Batman makes his transition in the Batcave of course, while Superman makes his transition in a phone booth. Now obviously any of the costumed SuperHeroes have to make a defined transition before they can venture out into the public eye, but even some SuperHeroes that were not *costumed* in the usual sense still observed some special ceremony. Apache Chief and the Wonder Twins, for example, both have brief incantations that trigger their special world.

In fact your transition signal can take the shape of many different things including something as simple as a mental incantation of your own, or perhaps a "Do Not Disturb" sign on the door to your study. You could even use a hidden folder on your computer that signals to your mind: "Hey—now we make the move." In this example your special computer folder might have links to your secret resources; or maybe it is a business on the side that you've been building; or maybe it's the blueprints for a real secret entrance that you are building next Tuesday. I don't know... after all, it's your secret!

The idea I am getting at here is that yes, you should have fun with it (like all things), but also that this is about *ceremony*. And believe it or not, implementing some sort of ceremony will really help with your SuperHero venture. If nothing else, it will definitely help solidify your transition to the special world, and right now, that's where all the action is.

Remember: this is your secret place, and that can mean anything from a hidden garden down a long path, or even a simple shoe box with your prized possessions in it. And if this sounds a little bit like something you may have done as a child, well, that's a good thing.

Like all the processes in this book so far, and all of the sections in this chapter, whatever you pick should be something sustainable. It shouldn't be too big of a challenge for you to actually trigger this transition as often as you choose.

INNER SANCTUM

Your inner sanctum is the place where you will go for peace and calm. Many use it for deep thought or meditation as well. If you are fortunate enough to have the space in your home, dedicate an entire room to this purpose. If you live in an apartment, a studio, a dorm room, or even share a room, you can still create this space for yourself. First decide how you will section off this area. Consider using a screen to mark off just a corner, for example. When I visited India it was so interesting to see how they used the strategic placement of whatever small screen, or even pieces of a scarf, they could find to create a small shrine as a place for worship. Get creative with this project!

The inner sanctum is so very important to the success of a SuperHero. Superman has his Fortress of Solitude (though it is far away, it is easily accessible to him, since he can fly). Batman retires to the Batcave for his solitude and focus (though it seems he is always alone, even on the streets of Gotham). Sherlock Holmes would sit and think for all hours of the night with just his pipe (and so it would seem that his inner sanctum was inside his head). In all cases however the emergence from their allegorical cave brings with it fresh insights and clearer vision. Perhaps, too, in your life.

> **" Your inner sanctum can be a place for you to re-energize and gather yourself.**

Your inner sanctum can be a place for you to re-energize and gather yourself. If you associate it (or its special configuration, as above) with immediate peace and calm, it will have always have this effect on you.

In whatever space you choose, there are many ways to bring about your desired effect. Start with what calms you in your life already, and try to have some instance of it there. Another effective method is to use a particular scent for only this special space. Don't use it anywhere else, or it won't create the right effect. You can do this in many ways. Try burning incense, lighting a scented candle, or even having a bowl of potpourri if you like. The idea is to use a scent (since smell is the strongest sense tied to recalling a memory) to create a positive association within you.

Some people might make their inner sanctum full of things that are white because of its association with purity. Consider white walls, a white pillow, or even white candles. You may also want to have some sort of means to get comfortable in this area. You don't have to overdo it: one pillow might suffice. It doesn't take a lot, it takes only thought. In Shinto-ism for example, there may be only a high shelf and a few sacred items. Either way, think it through.

Other than your standing meditation (taught in Chapter 10), you can also practice your power of meditation here. Use this area to make yourself completely calm. Live inside of yourself for a period of time every day. Let everything else fall away. This practice will help cultivate an enormous amount of patience and calm within you that you can learn to access whenever you become stressed.

HALL-OF-FAME

Oh this one is quite outwardly exciting, unlike the last one which is a bit more... introspective, shall we say? The Hall-of-Fame is great for the boost we all need sometimes when things get us down. Believe me, even SuperHeroes get the blues. And, oh man, when they do they certainly are a miserable lot. They're giving up their powers, leaving their friends and girlfriends behind, even sulking their days away off in some far distant place (Spider-Man, Wolverine, and Superman, respectively). Even Jason Bourne was a bit whiny in the movies with his whole "poor-me routine," although he seemed to just beat up people as a quick-fix. Anywho...

Back to the fun and happy time of the Hall-of-Fame. We are talking about pure show-off time here folks! These are happy memories—indulge! What have you achieved in your life? Name it and then write it down, right now as you read this. Do you have any trophies from playing sports when you were younger? Perfect attendance awards? Honor Roll? What are you proud of about yourself today? Everyone has something. Maybe it's just your decision to become a SuperHero! That's fantastic! Let's just run with that! The hall-of-fame is about honoring the amazing person that you are.

The idea here is to create a part of your house that is dedicated exclusively to celebrating you. Even if you don't have any physical representations of the things of which you are proud, make some! Seriously! And please hear this, it's important. Even if all you do is just go to 123certificates.com, type in your name, and your achievements, and print them out, that's enough.

Do the same thing with your Diploma. Why not? You earned it. Put it in a frame and hang it on your wall. If you are artistic, you may even want to draw or paint a little trophy. Do whatever it takes to have an area where you can look at and recall your achievements. I promise you it is worth it.

NOTABLE ACCOMPLISHMENTS:

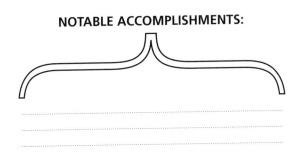

What does this have to do with being a SuperHero you ask? Only everything! Having a place that lets you recall all of your achievements and everything about yourself of which you are proud helps to maintain your confidence. Steve Stronghold (The Commander in Disney's Sky High) has one, Batman has one, Tony Stark has one too, though not actually of his SuperHero exploits, just of all his other conquests in both business and academics. Next time you are in your doctor's office, take a look up on their wall... what do you think all those certificates are up there for?

If you don't have space on a wall, or a separate trophy room, or maybe you have chosen to be a work SuperHero (like a Freelancer), you can always keep what I like to call a Smile File. This is kind of like the same thing, only more portable. Whenever anyone sends you a nice e-mail, or compliments you on a job well done, you simply print out a copy and keep it in your desk drawer or maybe even a folder. Then... whenever you need a boost, you simply pull out your Smile File and marvel at all your great work. This also helps with resumes, promotions, and raises to remind both you and your bosses of all your accomplishments (and not just in your own words, but theirs as well).

You may not feel like this is a very important step, or that you need a place like this in your life, but seriously, you may want to reconsider. A SuperHero maintains their confident disposition wherever possible. Having a place in your home reinforces this self-assured view of yourself. It helps cement your most positive attributes and allows them to flourish.

MOST WANTED LIST

This is another cool addition to your secret lair. All SuperHeroes have goals. We know this because they have made their life about completing some sort of mission. To keep themselves on track it would make sense that they kept an agenda of the things for them to undertake next. I think there is a mistaken sense about SuperHeroes that they just go from one tragic scene to the next, righting all wrongs, and finding themselves completely at the mercy of the day's events. I know people like this. They don't have a very long shelf-life. Having staying power means having to stay on track. So, having said that, let's talk about your Most Wanted List.

Now, obviously, yes... this can be exactly like the one the FBI uses if your goal as a Super-Hero is to catch criminals. In fact if you did this, you could just use theirs and not even have to make your own. But a Most Wanted List can also be about something more. What is it that you most want? Questions like "What goals do you want to achieve?"; "What villains do you want to catch?"; "What items do you most want to own?" are all good considerations. Basically, a Most Wanted List is really a "what's next on the agenda" list.

If you have made it this far in the book, you should probably have a very clear conception of your answers to all of these questions. You can be firing off the answers to these questions out-loud, quickly and confidently, or at the very least, writing them down.

MY MOST WANTED LIST

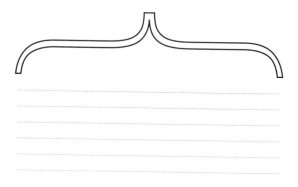

Now that your answers to these questions are clear, it's time to bring it into focus. Some people use a vision-board for this. They cut out pictures of everything they want and attach them to a large board to keep in their forefront. Personally, I'm not that creative. I like to find pictures on the Internet and make them the desktop image of my computer. Sometimes I even make them a slide show in my BlackBerry.

Either way, the goal is to find pictures that represent the details of how you imagine your future. Then you cut them out and tack them to a cork board, or something similar. The biggest issue people seem to have with this though is not the making. It's the displaying and sharing. Let me reassure you, it really is ok to display this in your house. You can even do so with pride.

Listen, it's ok to want things. Making a list just helps you visualize your future. Whatever your goals are, this is an important step because it helps maintain your focus on your goals. And focus is what will bring them to you. To this end, some people make a list of their goals and then carry them around in their purse or wallet. At any given time they know exactly what they want, and this makes them significantly more likely to get it.

The power of your focus and the clarity of your vision are major players in getting what you want. Give it a go... you won't regret it.

GADGET GALLERY

This one is a nice to have, though it may not work for everyone. Have you ever seen those movies where the hero (often a guy) opens up some wall and behind it is this huge rack of weapons? In a way, that's kind of what this is. Now there are of course some differences because not everybody maintains (or would even want to maintain) a complete arsenal in their house, but the idea remains a constant.

What are the tools of your trade? Maybe you have climbing gear because you are a rescue worker. Can you see how it would help to have a separate staging area for all of your equipment? Perhaps even an area to don your costume, if you have chosen to wear one. Iron Man has a special area in which he keeps his gear, because it is so specialized. Many of the other SuperHeroes in fact do the same thing, especially those that have dual identities.

Even if your SuperHero type keeps you connected to a computer, there may be certain resources or books on which you draw for difficult situations... whatever it is, you may find it useful to cordon off an area that remains dedicated to the job at hand.

This is especially important if you depend on your gear to protect you or to save your life. SCUBA Divers, Police Officers, Mountain Climbers... very different jobs, yet all of them have a huge respect for their gear because they have a real need to count on it to save their lives, or the lives of someone else. Now certainly this will vary, especially if you don't have very much gear, but you may find it cool to invest in one of those metal briefcases that you see in the movies and keep your special, tactical equipment in there. Plus, it adds to the mystique and fun of actually being a SuperHero—so why the heck not?

DANGER ROOM

I think I like this one the best (well, except maybe for that whole Offshore Bank Account thing—that's just way cool). Seriously I have to tell you, growing up reading about the X-Men and everything they went through in the original Danger Room really made me want to be able to go through the same thing. It really put them to the test. I even came up with an idea using overhead projectors and paint-ball guns that is being put together even as I write this.

As cool as that will be once it is complete, here is one exciting concept that you can actually use today that also came from this: a War Room. I can imagine high-level executives getting great value out of this. Basically the war room idea goes like this (and even has a few variations). A business type SuperHero (the Freelancer) rallies his troops (if you will) by calling them into the war room. Right away they know there is some serious projects afoot. If you happened to notice that this is like combining the idea of the Secret Entrance, Ceremony, and the Special World, you are right on target. It also standardizes the idea of getting your game face on in a way that isn't too conventional.

By the way, there is no value to just renaming your current conference room. The moment you start holding pointless meetings about nothing in there, you have just destroyed any value that the place had to offer. Be warned.

Richard Branson, a personal hero of mine, uses the idea of a war room as well, although in his words he uses them to "tackle environmental problems and disease, bringing together global leaders to form the Elders—compassionate people who wield their huge influence for the good of humanity" (Business Stripped Bare. Branson. Virgin Books. 2008.).

Another way to use the idea of the Danger Room is the idea of the gymnasium as used by Batman. Basically it's like an indoor obstacle course that he uses to condition himself for all the challenges he finds while swinging from rooftops and doing battle with enemy bad guys. It is an arena of pure focus. Notably, he also has the huge bank of computers in a separate area of the Batcave which also helps to focus him on the task at hand. In this way he bridges two areas (the mental and the physical). Where possible, we can learn from this example of preparation and I will cover this more in Chapter 17.

In a similar vein, the Construct Program used by Neo and Morpheus in the aforementioned movie The Matrix was a great example of this concept. They fought the way you would in a dojo, they strategized the way you would in a war room, and they loaded up their gear the way you would in an armory (though this last one plays more to the idea of the Gadget Gallery above, it works here because they still maintained them as separate locations with just the push of a button).

The main thrust of the idea behind this, and in fact most of the concepts in this book, is to play up the elite in your life... the elite ideas, the elite methods, the whole mentality—all of it. Just play it up to the highest extent that you can. Be big, be fantastic, be elite. And you know, it's funny, but the more you do that, the more real it all gets.

OFFSHORE BANK ACCOUNTS

Obviously.

Your Mission, Should You Choose to Accept It

A FIRST LOOK AT FINDING ACTION, JACKSON

A First Look at Finding Action, Jackson

It takes great courage to shatter the silence with song. Let that resonate with you a little bit. Have you ever been in a place where everything was quiet? Not even an awkward or an uncomfortable quiet. Just quiet. Like a coffee shop, perhaps. As you look around everyone is pretty much just doing their own thing. In silence.

Imagine that this is the setting when you suddenly decide to open up with both lungs and sing out loud! Absolute happiness and joy reverberating from you with your arms open and spread out wide. I imagine you'd even be laughing at that point, although people around you might be a little put off. But can you see what I mean here? It does take a great amount of courage to shatter the silence with song! And of course, we're not talking about quietly asking the silence to maybe scoot over just a little bit so that you can sit next to it, but to really shatter it! To sing out; loud and proud. Think about doing this at the next coffee shop you are in. Doesn't it feel a little uncomfortable?

So why would you ever do this? Well, because that's what being a SuperHero is all about. Let me explain, and allow me to repeat a sentence from the beginning: It takes great courage to shatter the silence with song.

Well, if this is true, then you should know right now that it takes even more courage to stand up when we see an injustice being carried out. It's even harder still if this injustice does not affect you directly. But this is exactly what the SuperHero does: they speak out. They rise when no one else will, because someone should stand up, when someone else needs them to. They rise and they stand firm.

We mere mortals have a bit of a habit sometimes of not standing up (or even standing out for that matter). It is almost a basic tenet of organized society going all the way back to the beginning, so says social thinker and philosopher Rousseau. But standing up or not, you must admit that there are, everywhere around you, so many things that you would change if only you could. If only you had the voice. Well I am here to tell you that you do have that voice. You have it, and it is right there inside you, right now and it is waiting—no, begging—to come out. Free it. Free that voice and that indecision and rise, my faithful friend, rise... and in so doing become that Hero, that Champion, that this oppressed and downtrodden world so greatly desires.

Do you want to be a SuperHero? Do you want to rise up above the rest in order to right all of the wrong that you see happening every single day around you? Would you like some real practice at fighting injustice wherever you see it? Then sing out! It is absolutely essential.

Begin to sing out in public in the most booming, projected voice you can muster (and yes t will also help you to cultivate a great SuperHero voice as well). When you have this skill completely under your control, when you can sing out and raise the spirits of those around you, then you will also be ready to speak out with confidence. It is not a challenge to be taken lightly. But it will absolutely transform you.

MISSION CONTROL, WE HAVE A PROBLEM

Ok, so let's make a checklist of where we are at this moment:

- ☑ You have all of the training you have deemed necessary
- ☑ You have your Powers (and maybe an optional theme song)
- ☑ You are ready, willing, and able to use them
- ☑ You have your mission statement
- ☑ You have your secret lair
- ☑ You have all your tools at the ready
- ☑ You are focused and ready
- ☑ You will stand up at a moment's notice and sing out loud
- ☐ You have your first mission

Uh-oh, you know what that means. It looks to me like somebody's checklist came up a little short today. I think it's time to grab ourselves a mission. Are you ready folks? Who's with me? Great! Now if only we had a way to get one... oh, wait a minute... what's this?

HAVING THE MISSION COME TO YOU

Let's talk about enrollment. This isn't the school type either. This is more like, um, let's call it: Name it, then Claim it. When you have a dream, or even a goal in mind, the more people you enroll in your accomplishing that goal, the more likely you are to hit it. This isn't a discussion about idle chatter either. Nor is it about bragging.

Let's look at it this way: when you are held accountable for something, you are more likely to do it, than when you are not being held accountable. So the question is, how many people have you enrolled in what you are doing? Do those around you know that you are now a SuperHero? Do they know that you started the program at least? Because if there is a group of people that know you started, then telling them that you finished is one way to drum up business, so to speak.

Honestly though, if you have followed all of the advice given, and I mean all of it, then

> **❝ There is no such thing as an accident. We are not victims here. We write our own roles.**

they will simply know by your actions. It's a fact. Your demeanor, the very way you carry yourself, will in fact speak more about you than any of your words ever could. More to the point, they will most likely recognize the change in you. And if I haven't said it by now: "we teach people how to treat us." This means that they will respond to you. The new you, the old you... it doesn't matter, they respond. You decide what it is they do and how they respond.

What all this really means is that if you are a SuperHero, then they will see it and fill the void where your missions should be. After following advice like this, in a world like today, having too few missions will be the least of your worries. But you first have to enroll people. At least the first few. Think of it as the Grand Opening of a new boutique... would you tell people about it? Just one person? Many people? It's the same thing here.

THE ACCIDENTAL PURIST (NOT PLANNING FOR EVERYTHING)

Much of this book has been about planning and goal-setting (and getting). This isn't to say that there isn't room for circumstance and spontaneity. Far from it. However, luck happens when preparation meets opportunity. In other words: prepare. Now, having said that, remember the exercise about singing out? One of the largest lessons to come out of that experience is leaving your comfort zone. It's big because nothing exciting ever happens when you are inside a box. Change your thinking, change your circumstances. You can attract literally anything to your life. Literally... anything.

Have you ever known someone who things just seem to happen for (or to)? This section is called The Accidental Purist for a reason. There is no such thing as an accident. We are not victims here. We write our own roles. We attract our own, unique circumstances.

So if you crave the happenstance, have it. You can be there, and it will happen... anywhere really. But you must really be there. Don't just be at a place and maybe thinking about something else. Focus. I mean really be there. Be present to it. This hearkens back to the various musings on Consciousness again but it is honestly quite applicable to this section as well.

I don't know any other way to get this point across, except with a few examples.

There was a time in my life when I was transitioning, so to speak. I had to change much about who I was... everything, in fact, and I do mean everything. I had to redefine who was as a person. Honestly: I simply did not like who I was. I didn't like my name, my attitude, my upbringing, my job, my life, my level of schooling, any of it... Since I refused to keep living that way, everything had to go. So I began a process of change.

I rented a small place for a year and cut myself off from the world. I did a lot of soul-searching and reading during that time and I was lucky to have made a few new friends in my life that saw where I was and offered me direction. A funny thing began to happen though, and that is the focus of this section.

During this time I realized that I wanted to be someone who helped people. I wanted to be more of an empath. All of a sudden, accidents kept popping up around me—literally. Car accidents, human accidents, you name it. They of course were not accidents. It was an interesting time.

There were children in the streets, there were mothers, crying... they happened right in front of me. Once, while sitting in my studio, something said: "Get up. Go now." So I left. A few minutes later I saved a kid from an attacker that broke his ribs and was literally trying to kill him. I did it anonymously.

Months later we were reunited. His mother and sister were there. We all cried when we realized who each other was. It was spectacular.

Magical things began to happen. People I had never met began approaching me with gifts; with conversation; with questions. We talked at length and never spoke again. Wherever I was needed, I just was. I have no other explanation.

Be open to it. The things you want to bring about will come about if you just focus your energies in that direction. Whatever it is you focus on, you become.

RADAR LOVE

How else might you find a mission? Well this section will show you the electronic devices and tools that will help you to do just that. Don't worry if you aren't a gadget freak, or even very computer savvy. Many of the things listed below are very simple (and also user-friendly) so that will make things much easier for you. Also, there are a bunch of other sections here that don't use technology... so again, don't worry. Just find wherever you are comfortable, and start there.

The world alert map at hisz.rsoe.hu/alertmap is a thing of beauty. Well...actually it's a little scary, but I think that's a good thing considering the topic. This is literally a map of whatever disaster is going on in the world at any given moment. Try and take that in for a minute.

As I write this there is a Biological Hazard in America, a vehicle accident in Canada, a landslide in Colombia, an earthquake in the Indonesian Archipelago, a tropical storm in India, and a terror attack in the Sudan. Take your pick, SuperHeroes.

If your next thought is "Whoa," and your next question is "How do I keep track of it all?" never fear, your answer is here. It's called Pingie. Funny name, I know, but a great tool, none-the-less. It takes that map and feeds it to your phone in little tiny bites that you can actually handle. And yes, I do vouch for it, and in fact have it on me all the time. It is quite common in fact for me to look down at my Blackberry and see some major disaster in the works, and think to myself: wow—if I had a jet, and that were my mission (which usually it isn't), I could head over there right now. I wonder if Superman does that? "Sorry Lois, I'll be right back."

Since I live in Los Angeles, I also use tools that are much closer to home. The Fire Department for one... Twitter, for another (even Amber Alerts can now be sent to you). In fact, more than any other publicity campaign or poster I have ever seen, the LAFD Twitter feed has made me an absolute believer in those guys (and gals).

I also get these on my phone at 2 in the morning, but when I do, I am always amazed at how incredible these people are. Since I have been watching, they have been called to a storm in Louisiana, fires across the county (obviously), overturned vehicles, and (most surprising to me), aircraft on approach to LAX that may not be going to land safely. I have to say, this last one is the most crazy of all—knowing in advance that this plane may be about to crash, but then having to wait it out and see... wow. Thank you LAFD.

Now of course there is an old school version of this, and yes, I suppose police scanners are great for this sort of thing. But really... I know nothing about them. Somehow it seems a little before my time. If it helps, the LAPD is considering a Twitter feed as well. I don't know if they will use it as much as their fire department brethren, but if they want all the good press, it may be a good idea.

Another way, in the land of electronica, to find a mission is by joining online groups. I used to be a member of some online, Internet Police thing. I wasn't a cop (in fact I had no authority whatsoever), but the site was there and I think we were supposed to look after some things. Sorry to say I have no idea if it is still around, but I can suggest Facebook, Yahoo, or Google groups as ways to link up with people who share a common goal. Just a thought.

One of the more creative ideas I might suggest is elance. It is a website on which people list their services so that others can bid. Think of it like placing an online classified ad (which also may work). Now for elance it is usually programming jobs, but I have seen other things on there as well, and who knows: maybe they need a category for a SuperHero in search of a mission. Check it out.

The easiest recipe of course is to just sign up with all the things listed above and have them sent to your phone. You can always have it with you, and you will always know when and where your services are needed. Call it a hunch, but I bet that if you put your services out there... someone will take you up on your offer.

SEEING A NEED & SAVING THE DAY

How is this part different than the previous mission-makers? Well, by way of explanation let me point out that this section actually goes in two directions. The first is the "seeing a need" part. Now yes this was covered somewhat in your mission statement, or perhaps your vision statement, if you opted to add that portion, but here we go a little further. In that section you identified your passion and hopefully wrote it down. The key point here though, is that now you've seen the need that you go fill it. It's a tried and true system. You saw the problem; it's your life's mission to fix it… you do so. Sounds like a plan to me.

Call it your niche, if you like. But whether a niche or just an itch, if there happens to be a need, and your eyes are trained to see it, then you get to be the one who fills it. You still have to move on it of course, and that's where the next part comes in.

The second part is the "saving the day" part. Now, yes, this is somewhat like the accidental pursuit section above, but differs in at least one key area. That section was about intention where this section is more about action. A SuperHero needs both. In the other methods in this chapter, your intention was made known (to your friends in the first section, and to the universe in the second section) and you prepared yourself for certain inevitabilities. In this one, when a situation appears in front of you, you act. You don't hesitate. You do what you know only you can do. This is the "saving the day" part, and this is why all of the preparation has been so very important. If you can sing out for fun, you will at least be able to call out to others for support in your mission. If you have trained, you will be ready. This is what you can do; this is what you must do. It may in fact be the very moment for which you have been waiting.

On Doing Battle

A FIRST LOOK AT THE FIGHT OF YOUR LIFE

A First Look at The Fight of Your Life

In the section before this you were tasked with standing up against an injustice. It would be irresponsible of me to leave you standing there alone. Are we not SuperHeroes? Do we not each stand together against our demons? Because I cannot be there physically with you, I would like to offer you some guidance instead.

When engaged in any battle your primary obligation is to triumph. This isn't only about a physical fight. Will it apply there? Yes, absolutely. Does it apply elsewhere? Also yes.

Try to see the following pieces of information solely for what they are: helpful advice for the situation at hand. Whether you are in a legal battle, a struggle for your own health and survival, or a corporate battle in the working world, try to understand the possible applications for what you are about to read. And if the battle is important enough for you to have changed your entire life around in order to become its supreme challenger, then I wish you tremendous luck as well.

WHEN A STICK OF GUM CAN SAVE YOUR LIFE

This section is the most important in the book when it comes to practical applications. It's about preparation. I will beg, plead, and implore you not to go into battle unprepared. I would beseech you, but I am not exactly sure how one does that.

But how does gum fit into this equation? Well it's tricky to be sure, but it has a lot to do with preparation. It's also about using everything at your disposal to give you the added edge over your opponent. If you knew you were going in for one last round, wouldn't you want to give the absolutely strongest performance you could give? I think you would. Here's a trick the bad guys don't know yet (which is why I didn't put it in the weapons section).

It's called Stay Alert gum and it has some interesting properties. The testimonials on the website are letters from Congress. The testing has been done by a joint task force of scientists from both the US and Canada on soldiers over periods of 28 hours where they aren't allowed to sleep. It is clinically proven to improve both mental and physical abilities, marksmanship, and vigilance. It is used by the military in situations where operational readiness means the difference between life or death, endorsed by the National Academy of Sciences, and it can be had for about $8.00. That's right: I said eight bucks.

If you think that is crazy... just wait until you read the (very specific) usage instructions:

CANADIAN MILITARY JOURNAL • WINTER 2003 - 2004

Chewing one or two sticks of gum for five minutes, then discarding, has been shown to deliver 85 percent of the total caffeine dose in each stick. Each stick contains 100 mg of caffeine.

➡ **1. FOR MENTAL PERFORMANCE:** In a rested state, start with one stick and chew more as needed to maintain alertness. In a sleep deprived state, no more than two sticks every two hours for up to six hours should be consumed.

➡ **2. FOR PHYSICAL PERFORMANCE:** Chew two sticks for five minutes followed immediately by another two sticks prior to beginning the initial activity. Re-dose with one stick after six hours for subsequent hard work.

➡ **3. PHYSICAL FOLLOWED BY MENTAL PERFORMANCE:** Use four sticks initially for physical performance prior to initial assault. To maintain cognitive performance after the physical effort, chew one stick as required.

➡ **4. MENTAL FOLLOWED BY PHYSICAL PERFORMANCE:** In the rested state, chew a total of four sticks within two hours of the exercise. In the sleep-deprived state, where multiple sticks of gum would already have been chewed within a four-hour period, additional sticks of gum may not be required for optimizing physical performance.

➡ **5.** Regular caffeine users may have to slightly increase their dose to achieve the same benefits.

➡ **6.** Do not exceed 10 sticks in a 24-hour period.

DO NOT USE THIS PRODUCT IF YOU ARE OVERLY SENSITIVE TO CAFFEINE

What other interesting things fall into being prepared? How about taking an improv class in order to learn to think on your feet? It is fun, and the added benefits are surprising, to say the least. Take up the game of Go. It is an amazing game of strategy and skill, and shows you that even the most simple things can have meaning. Join a gymnastics class (trust me, it's never too late), you will gain mobility and add to your flexibility. Both very much needed.

If you haven't yet guessed, this is all about training and preparing in ways you may not have considered. Gum is a funny way to start, it's true. But it has value and helps explain the point. Have fun with your preparation, but definitely prepare.

BATTLE WITHOUT HONOR OR HUMANITY

Now you understand the value of preparation. But what would you do if when I said the word "go," your fight immediately began? How would you handle yourself? What would you do to survive? What is the one concrete thing you could do right now, that would help you win, even if you weren't prepared? Your only option might just be to focus with everything you have, and then hope for the best. In The Judo Textbook (Nishioka, 1979, Black Belt Communications) an athlete is compared to a kamikaze when he can "commit himself mentally, emotionally and physically to winning, even when that contest may result in his death.... It is one of the most important factors in the makeup of a champion" (154).

So why is this section named after a song from the movie Kill Bill? Because a SuperHero is called to great heights my friend, and if you should happen to fall from there... well... let's just say you have a long way down to think about what happened. The world is watching you and I'll let you in on a little secret: we really don't want you to fall. We want you to succeed, and overcome those things that go bump in the night. We need you. Quite honestly, I need you.

I want to know that the world has a new generation of heroes and they are not happy with the way things are. If you are on the side of hope, if you stand for justice, then bring the fight to the enemy with such a force that you will not be repelled. We ask that you battle the enemy this way, that you then shall triumph, and that you bring home that great boon for which we have all been waiting.

DIE LIKE A SAMURAI

And what happens when you bring that focus? Then you face the opponent as would the Samurai of feudal Japan. Now, before you get the wrong idea, I am not suggesting you run out and just die. Because let's face it: that would just be lame. Besides, sometimes it takes more courage to live for something than it does to simply die for it. So what am I saying?

D.T. Suzuki says it better, so let's begin there, shall we? In his book Zen and Japanese Culture (Suzuki, 1970, Princeton University), he tells the story of a run-in between a Tea Master and Ruffian. That's a bad guy. Well, as you may have guessed, a person whose life has been completely focused on serving tea, may not quite be ready for a sword fight to the death with a trained swordsman. You would have guessed correctly.

In the story the Tea Master asks to postpone the duel until the morning and the bad guy agrees. Afterwards, the Tea Master finds a teacher and asks him how he can die like a samurai. He knows he won't survive a fight with this person, so he at least wants to die with dignity. The teacher asks him to pour him some tea while he thinks it over. When he witnesses the incredible focus of this man in the act of tea preparation, he immediately knows the answer.

He tells him to arrive at the battle site and put himself into that same mental state (the one he had when performing the Tea Ceremony) and to perform each action there with that same care, that same grace, in fact that complete Love. Move directly, maintain your focus and your intense concentration, hold your calm and poise. Until death, this person is as a guest at your table. Raise your sword over your head and wait. When you hear the yell of his attack: bring down your sword and cut. Most likely you will both be dead.

Don't fear young reader, for there is a happy ending (when I first heard this as a kid I was worried as well). The next morning when the two faced each other, the Tea Master did exactly as he was told. The other man looked into his calm and focused eyes and knew immediately that this was not the same man he had faced the day before. His will was immediately broken and he conceded the fight, right there on the spot.

It is about focus, but it is also about committing to the very end of a thing. Remember, this isn't only about sword fights and samurai. Whatever the battle, have your clearest focus, your battle plans, and your complete dedication to winning with you at all times. Or at least be able to call it up when you need to.

HOW TO OVERCOME, AND HOW TO WIN

So what have we learned? The most committed, wins. Said differently: the clearest conception of the outcome will win in any confrontation, relationship, or interaction. Now of course if you are a retired Navy SEAL Officer you might say it as: "Unrelenting, violent aggression in the face of adversity. It's how you get through it, [.... because] only the most committed wins. Winning in this business... means living." Or, if you are a UFC Cage Fighter in the battle of their career, you might simply say "I'm gonna whoop Chuck's ass" and focus only on that. And guess what? In both cases you'll win.

The point for both is the same. Don't over-imagine, don't wander or worry too much. Just focus. Intently. Whatever the battle, if you are in it, you must absolutely overwhelm your opposition. Make this objective your only focus. That's it.

In the "Water" section of A Book of Five Rings (Harris, Overlook, 1974) Musashi (quite possibly the world's greatest swordsman) says you must always focus on the cut. "If you think only of hitting, springing, striking, or touching the enemy, you will not be able to actually cut him. More than anything, you must be thinking of carrying your movement through to cutting him."

By the way, I certainly apologize if the statements here sound rather hostile. This isn't about warmongering. As I have mentioned, these words do not only apply to physical confrontation, and thankfully most people reading this book will never find themselves with that need anyway. This doesn't mean however that the concepts won't apply to other challenges in life. They absolutely will and they quite often do.

All we are discussing here is the physical application of your mental desire; it's the tangible creation of your indomitable willpower... because wanting it, is not enough. Whether your battle is in the boardroom or the war room, the instruction is the same. If you want something, you go after it and you use everything in your power to get it. You do not rest until you have it.

Make no mistake: it is very challenging. I struggled with this book (and many other things in my life as well), when I could have simply chosen to overwhelm my task with an unreasonable response. I could have thrown so much effort at it that it had no choice but to submit. But I didn't, and my book (and my life) slogged on because of it. I will be taking this lesson to heart, I promise you.

ON THE CARE AND FEEDING OF STRONG LANGUAGE

Earlier in the book I instructed you to "Speak Strongly—Use SuperHero Verbiage." What does this mean exactly? How is it that a SuperHero would speak? Let me reuse a little of that here and see if I can offer you something as a guide.

Quite literally our words shape our reality. The more richly you are able to interact with your environment, the greater the effect you can have on it. Also, our words have a way of attracting people to us that share our points of view. As a SuperHero you must therefore use your words in the most powerful way you know how.

You must be bold, yes. But you must also speak boldly. The Silver Surfer, for example uses language easily suited for nobility. Now obviously, that won't work for everyone, it won't work in every scenario, nor is it what I am actually suggesting you do. No, what I am suggesting you do is to use the most powerful verbiage you can that is appropriate for the situation. Let me give you some examples.

The first example is a song from the musical Man of la Mancha. Call me crazy, but the version of "The Impossible Dream" by Richard Kiley is absolutely awe-inspiring. You can read some of it below, but try to actually listen to a copy to understand what I mean. As an added bonus, his voice is right on target to be the booming sound for which a SuperHero might strive.

> **To dream... the impossible dream**
>
> **To fight... the unbeatable foe**
>
> **To bear... with unbearable sorrow**
>
> **To run... where the brave dare not go**
>
> **To right... the unrightable wrong**
>
> **To love... pure and chaste from afar**

To try... when your arms are too weary

To reach... the unreachable star.

This is my quest, to follow that star...

No matter how hopeless, no matter how far...

To fight for the right, without question or pause...

To be willing to march into Hell, for a Heavenly cause...

The next example has to do with leading people. In many cases the SuperHero is quite easily looked up to. People see this shining emblem, this great beacon of hope, and they naturally fall under its spell. If it is your job to lead people, one thing to use to your advantage is your language. The stronger, more powerful, and even more evocative your language, the better the result. Without it, you may quite naturally see things fall completely apart.

To paraphrase the Academy Award winning movie U-571 (Universal, 2000)

> *"Don't you dare say what you said to the boys back there again: 'I don't know.' The Captain always knows what to do, even when he doesn't. Those three words will kill a boy just the same as a depth charge."*

The point to this one is that not only does uncertainty reduce morale, but in the wrong situation it can also be deadly. Use strong verbiage, and watch the results speak for themselves.

Yet another example of strong language would be how ridiculously powerful is the language that police use when they are on a raid. In watching some training exercises for drug interdiction operations in the western Pacific, I was continually struck by how powerful the shouted commands were, yet they were also so simple and direct (and this is key). This unceasing barrage of such strong verbal attacks kept everyone continually off-balance and unable to organize a defense. The "bad guys" seemed overwhelmed and the ops went off smoothly. It was amazing.

It is also amazing how powerful the shouted voice of a recognized authority figure actually is to us. I would imagine it stems from childhood and the consequences ingrained within us back then, but it is still an awesome power none-the-less.

On a simpler note, in your doings with others, don't be wishy-washy with your decisions. Stand firm in them. Eventually your ability to make these decisions will get better. Also don't be afraid to change up the verbiage you use around them now. As I have mentioned, we teach people how to treat us. Show them that you are stronger now; and let them hear it as well.

Antithesis on the Rise

A FIRST LOOK AT THE DARK SIDE

A First Look at The Dark Side

Being a SuperHero is not about being perfect. Tony Stark (among others) has certainly shown us that. We all have weaknesses. It is the nature of our humanity. But that's not a bad thing. It's quite possibly our best thing. Nietzsche says (in paraphrase anyway) that man is remarkable because we are a bridge, not a destination. We are on our way to becoming something much more amazing. Something so incredible that our entire race will be transformed. Use this moment. Take your weaknesses, carry along your dark side—hell embrace it! And walk with me along this bridge that is our lives. I promise you that the extra weight you must carry will well be worth it at journey's end when you find you must rally both sides of your spirit in order to overcome. Let us go now, that we may learn more about these areas in our lives; that we understand our fragilities, and then finally that we come to better terms with them.

Do you remember the song from the last chapter about your quest, your trials, and your tribulations? I want to bring your attention to one particular part of that song. Specifically the line: "to be willing to march into hell for a heavenly cause." This will begin our discussion of your dark side.

> **66 ...humans are a funny sort of creature. If all of our problems were overcome we would likely cease to function.**

There will always be a "Hell" to oppose your heavenly cause, but you mustn't fear. Why must this thing exist? Because humans are a funny sort of creature. If all of our problems were overcome we would likely cease to function.

We grow only by overcoming our previous limitations. We only build muscle by first tearing it down. We only learn when we are confronted with the things we do not know. It is our struggle that provides us the most benefit, not our easy victories.

Now having said that, I am not talking about losing. When we lose, well... we lose. It is our struggle, combined with our eventual win, that provides us the power and even the desire to get back in there and struggle again. It is why we continue. Winning and struggle are the fuels we use and they are great motivators.

On a funny side note, this is also why we create our own little drama here and there. We need something to push against. If we have no other structured resistance (like school or perhaps complex tasks at work, or anything that we can continually work towards) we feel stagnant. All life is defined by growth. Therefore if you are not growing and living then you are dying. Most of us have a problem with just laying down and dying of course and so we provide our own hurdles that we can then overcome and leave behind as a symbol of our own growth. It isn't usually the best sort of growth for us however, which is why the unstructured don't grow as quickly as others.

Now to get back on track: Yes... you do have a dark side. You do have weaknesses. But those are good things (once you learn to work with them) so please move your seat-backs to their full, upright position, and let's set out together (with our weaknesses in tow) to integrate both of those sides into one Supreme Being: our new SuperHero.

CHOOSING YOUR KRYPTONITE

Your Kryptonite is something that makes you weak. In the world of Superman, Kryptonite is a metal from the planet Krypton where Superman was born. It weakens him and causes him to lose his powers whenever he comes across it. But let us consider this more closely: why should it be something from his home planet which weakens him? Would we not all have a Kryptonite then?

Is there something about your home life or past that makes you feel not up to par? Don't worry, you're not alone. We all have something crazy in our past. It's more important to make peace with it though, than to simply dwell on it, or try to conceal it. Maybe your weakening comes from an idea or a memory. Maybe it's not even something physical. Either way being honest with yourself and identifying your areas of weakness will help you to overcome them.

So why would somebody ever choose their own Kryptonite? Doesn't it exist already? Let's start off with "the enemy you know, is better than the one you don't." Let's also remember that, by and large, we create our own reality. It is ok for you to choose what makes you weak; and it certainly is better than feeling you have no choice.

Basically you can choose whatever Kryptonite you like. This gives you the advantage of knowing how to prepare for the time when your Kryptonite appears. You can literally practice in advance because you will see the signs well before the event ever happens. This also gives you more control over the consequences since you already knew it was about to show up. You remain the master, even over your weaknesses. It's really powerful... check it out.

UNDERSTANDING YOUR ARCH-ENEMY

Your arch-enemy is your opposing force, but that doesn't mean it is just a simple matter of good vs. evil. In fact, opposite forces exist everywhere. Consider the forces of yin and yang, dark and light, two-in-a-bowl soup, or even up and down. While these things do oppose each other, they also complement each other. Let's take a look at this point as it relates to you.

Yes, your arch-enemy may oppose you, but what about all the help they provide? After all, what is it that drives a person to make the world a better place, if not the things within it that they perceive as negative? This is why you must learn to integrate your dark side, and not just push it away. Besides, all sun makes desert. Complementing forces make something whole, and this is true inside of you as well.

Now of course, exactly what or whom your arch-enemy turns out to be, depends upon your mission, your goals, and the SuperHero type you have chosen. But the form isn't really as important as you might think. Your arch-enemy is a symbol of what stands against you. For example, if your mission is to fly into outer space, your arch-enemy may just be gravity. Better to know it's there and work around it than to try to overlook it.

Another way to label this concept is with the idea of your shadow. It is your own, more literal, dark side. One good example of the shadow-self at work is the person who lives to help the poor and homeless, but thinks for some reason that they must share that same fate, or live below the poverty line as well in order to do any real good. This a great example of someone not integrating their shadow into their life.

I ask you, would Bill Gates have been able to give literally billions of dollars to charity if he were always poor and martyred? Would Oprah have been able to open schools and help entire communities if she wasn't the wealthy, and quite famous, person that she is? It's obvious.

By the way, like most of the things in this book so far, this concept isn't at all mine. In fact I don't know if it is really anybody's, but I do know that I first heard of it from derivatives of the work of Joseph Campbell. If the ideas ring true to you it may be because of their connection to the mono-myth stories. According to Campbell, it is only when the hero integrates the shadow, that he becomes whole. I won't get into it here, but some examples of integrating the shadow that you may have seen could have come from things like Star Wars, or the Matrix movies, perhaps.

So what happens if you fight against the idea of a shadow? Well because it is an opposing pressure that helps maintain the balance, you are really just feeding into it. You may have heard that "what you resist, persists." Why is that? Well it's a balance. How many times have you heard someone say to not focus on the negative so much? Or perhaps, where you put your focus is where you will eventually end up?

There's a reason they tell you to focus on the positive. To focus on the negative just gives it more energy and builds it up. To overcome it actually requires accepting it, coming to terms with it, or making your peace. Let's try a short story to explain it. Stop me if you've heard this one.

It has been said that there are two wolves fighting within us, that they are constantly fighting for dominance. The Good Wolf is truth, kindness, love, benevolence and joy. The Bad Wolf is lies, destruction, envy and anger. They are of equal power, yet they constantly fight. Do you want to know which will win? The one you feed.

If that one didn't help clarify it for you, then let's take another look back at the comic book world for a different viewpoint on the arch-enemy story. I submit for your approval: The Batman and The Joker. And if your arch-enemy really is just the personification of the things you push away within yourself, then I have to tell you, The Batman has some serious soul-searching to do. Let me illustrate.

Throughout their history Batman and The Joker have been wound together probably as tightly as any arch-enemies ever could be. They are at some points exactly the opposite while at other points exactly the same. Let's start with the opposite list because that task actually proves to be much easier.

* Batman cares about people. The Joker destroys them.
* Batman fights for good, while The Joker fights for... well The Joker fights for whatever it is that crazy people fight for.
* Batman is a stress case. The Joker: not so much.

But interestingly, they seem to share more similarities than they do differences.

* They both share a similar origin, in that they each had a normal life with people they loved.
* Both of them had that life taken away from them through criminal acts resulting in the death of their loved ones. (Many people don't know that the Joker lost his wife and unborn child, which helped to push him over the edge.)
* They both became irrevocably changed on that day and became larger-than-life costumed players on Gotham's expansive stage.
* They both basically run amok and do whatever they choose, whenever they choose.
* They both reach out to the other for validation (and in the past have tried to tempt the other into throwing in the towel to join their ranks).
* But perhaps most telling, they both have had many chances to kill each

other and neither will actually do it.

In fact, for all his bad-mouthing of The Joker, and all of his many "attempts" to rid Gotham of The Joker's murderous exploits, The Batman probably wouldn't kill The Joker even if his life depended on it. In fact, for Batman's life to make any sense at all, it probably depends on exactly the opposite. I mean seriously: The Joker raped Batgirl and then killed Robin, and you know what? He's still alive! I'm guessing we can be pretty certain that, no matter the circumstances, The Batman wants The Joker that way. (For more on that see our website.)

Either way, whether we are discussing comic book heroes or real life, we all have our dark past, and we all have our problems. You stand a much better chance at succeeding if you accept your flaws, make peace with your dark side, and (as Campbell has suggested) integrate your shadow. An arch-enemy doesn't have to be a stopping point. Let it instead become your new beginning. The greater the challenge, the higher you will have to rise in order to prevail, and the greater will be your victory when you eventually triumph.

NEVER THE NEMESIS

Now this however, this is a different story. Having an arch-rival is not the same thing as having a nemesis. An indeed it is the nemesis that I hope you must never face. The Oxford English Dictionary defines the nemesis as "the inescapable agent of someone's downfall, especially when deserved." And how does one actually get a nemesis, and then get completely defeated, you ask? Well, that's the easy part. All you have to do to is ignore the problem of the arch-enemy.

Now, interestingly enough, the secret to avoiding such a tragic downfall, and never having a nemesis defeat you, is also just as easy. All you have to do is integrate your shadow (your darker side, the side of you which you do not want to exist).

Think about it: if you don't put a stop to your arch-enemy, then you are leaving them free to do as they please and the first thing they are going to do is to grow, and consolidate their power. It's just like a game of chess, if you leave the other camp completely alone, you give them free-reign to set up shop in any way they choose. How do you think that game will end up for you? Not so good, trust me.

INTEGRATING THE SHADOW

Ok so now that you agree you have to do it, what's the first step? Well, according to Campbell, the shadow represents our "darkest desire, untapped resources, or rejected qualities." As a SuperHero, where might that come into play? I have a friend with a terrible temper.

She pretends it isn't there, but we all pretty much know it is. One suggestion for her would be not to deny this part of herself, but instead to harness it to help her overcome difficulties.

Another example would be friends or family from which you may have distanced yourself because of some argument or past history. What if they have the exact thing to help you in your hour of need? A well-integrated person would have the resources to triumph. A fearful or repressed person would not.

Here is an illustration so that you may better understand this concept. Let us suppose you are afraid of being mean to someone because of an event in your past. As a result, you are nice to literally every person, all the time. Sound great? Well the problem is that when you are nice to everyone, you aren't really being genuinely nice to anyone. Your actions have no value because you aren't doing it because you want to, you are doing it because you think you should. Also you're not honoring any real emotions that may rise up.

On the other hand, if you aren't afraid of it, you can be more direct with people about how you feel. For SuperHeroes, and mortals alike, this is a needed quality. Good luck with this, and every other section you have on your plate right now: I know it's a lot.

The good news is that the next chapter is the last, and if you've made it this far you have covered practically every topic needed to accomplish your goal. Again: good luck, and I will see you in the next chapter.

(PART IV)

⇩

The Aftermath

Leaving Your Mark for All Mankind

A FIRST LOOK AT THE LAST IMPRESSION

A First Look at the Last Impression

Before I jump in to this last section, I want to take a minute and congratulate you. I know I have done this more than once throughout this book and for all I know you may even be sick of it. I hope not. You have traveled far by following these steps and already the world is beginning to feel your presence. Quite honestly some of you have traveled even farther than have I at this moment, however... by the time you read this I will be rather far along on my own journey as well.

I look forward to meeting you in your travels, and I wish you every success. As a final note, anyone who has purchased this book and has undertaken the journey I describe here can contact me for personal guidance and I will help you in any way that makes sense.

OF MEMOIRS AND MEMORIES

This part is not what you changed, created, toppled, overcame, destroyed or built. It is not the thing itself... it is your story about it. The map is not the territory. How will it be told? Here, you decide. It is quite like the mythology section in that regard, though I suppose it is aimed more at you keeping a journal of your exploits, or chronicling your path and power to a world that is hungry for change. The world needs you, get out there and join it as a force for good.

On that note, interestingly enough, the world also wants to hear a great story. Let it be yours that they hear. What happy dreams will you give them at night? What fires of passion will you stir in their breast? Let them see your example that they may seek to emulate your efforts and become more than they currently know how to become. Lead the way for them. If it rings true enough I tell you they will read it!

Get a ghostwriter if you can't write it yourself. Say it into a voice recorder if you need to. Whatever you need to do to get your story out, do it. Take those steps. And by the way, if you didn't know it already: books pay! And sometimes they pay really well. If you need help trying to figure out how to write down your journey, again... you can call me and I may be able to help. If I can't help you directly I will most likely know someone who can. Give it shot.

SUPERMAN VS. THE HULK

There is a battle being waged, and it isn't one being sold in stores or available online. It is a very different type of battle and your entire future may hang in the balance. According to <u>The Marvel Universe</u> (Sanderson, 1996, Abrams) "within the unassuming everyman is a being of godlike might and nobility that serves the good of all humanity." This of course refers to the gallant and noble Superman and says that you can rise up and in so doing the world shall be the better for your actions and cast myriad praises at your feet.

At the other end of this battle, the far, far darker end, we have the lesson of The Incredible Hulk, namely "within everyman lies great destructive power propelled by uncontrollable rage and egotism that can destroy civilization and overwhelm everything noble in the human spirit" (Ibid). My question in this writing has been to determine which force you will serve. I have my hopes and they are placed squarely on the side of right, but the power is ultimately yours to wield. I have my own power, and have therefore chosen my own road.

Before you decide however, I would like to take a moment and offer a glimpse at what others have done with the same power.

What do you see when you look at Bosnia, Darfur, Rwanda, or Nazi Germany, if not that same "great destructive power" having its orgiastic feast on the blood of humanity? It seems to me a despicable, downward spiral of self-indulgence with the only stated purpose to be one of removing from the earth those that are labeled lower than oneself. And with that I ask you: if we continue down their same path then what is next for humanity?

Superman was never my favorite SuperHero, but I admire the things for which he stands. I find in them a certain security because if he believes in it, then maybe others believe in it also. He is like the protective blanket strung up as a fort across my bedroom that shields me from harm. My super blanket is the protection of my youth and it is one that I would like to extend to children everywhere.

The adult in me now wonders if there will be enough protective blankets to go around, and that is why I made the call. When you picked up the phone on the first page of the book, it may not have been me that you imagined on the other line, but I have called out to you none-the-less. Choose as you will. You now know where I stand. I hope that you will join me there.

YOUR SUPERHERO LEGACY

This is your lasting contribution, for why else become a SuperHero if you have no desire to effect things on a greater scale? Maybe you decided something in the mythology chapter? Maybe it has been building in you since page 1, or maybe even before you opened the book. It may just be that your desire for change and legacy is why you bought the book in the first place. I don't know. But I do know that if we have learned anything in this book so far it is that having goals and a tangible idea of where you want to go is the only way to reliably get there. So, as in all chapters before, let's write it down.

MY LEGACY CHECKLIST	A STATEMENT OF MY LEGACY
○ Charitable Foundation?	....
○ Drug-Free School ?	....
○ Successful Business ?	....
○	....
○	....
○	....

FINAL WORDS

Stop hiding. Every day that you wait, the earth is refused a taste of your power and beauty. Let me ask you: What will the world be missing if you don't give it 100 percent? The world needs you because there are already big bad villains out there with no one to oppose them. The world needs you because there are already things that go bump in the night, and like the character HellBoy, we need you to bump back. The world needs you because there are a million issues affecting millions of people, and nobody else seems ready to just pick one and join the fray. The world needs you because—Oh to hell with it—the world needs you: just get out there and do something!

Appendix 1

Movies, Books, and Music

MOVIES	BOOKS
The Matrix	How to Become a SuperHero
What the Bleep Do We Know?	The Navy SEAL Workout Book
Elektra	Jonathan Livingston Seagull
Equilibrium	OBEs in 30 Days
Pursuit of Happyness	Celestine Prophecy
The Secret	Mountains... A Child's Spiritual Reader
The Assignment	Lucid Dreaming
The Fountain	Lucid Living...
The Butterfly Effect	Emmanuel's Book... Cosmos
Batman Begins	Rolling Thunder... Weaponry
Phenomenon	Speed Reading Made Easy
Spy Game	Drive to Survive
MUSIC	
Man of La Mancha	Breakaway
The Impossible Dream	Kill Bill

Yet another completely fun section to go through: Books, Movies and Music! Ok, so what are we looking at here? Why these movies? Why these books? How do they actually relate to what your choices were in creating your own life?

Well, these are actually some fairly simple questions, and the answers are straightforward. These items were chosen because they all represent pathways to your new future. Further: all of them take the fog out of your journey. It doesn't have to be cloudy any more. The process needn't be an uncertain struggle, and the reason for this is simple: it's because you are the one who decides exactly what will be. So if you're not vague, your results won't be either. Now conversely, that isn't to say that they take away the mystery, because they don't. No, what they do is add back in the clarity.

Movies are an especially fun way to do the change-over as well because you get to watch it on screen and have all of these tiny little character twists affirming your direction and all the possibilities that await you. The books are the same way. Well, sometimes better depending on your ability to immerse yourself, and your level of attachment. They help to give you a part of the puzzle that you may not have had before. Sometimes it is even helpful to see the same piece of the puzzle from a completely different viewpoint.

You will also notice that the items (the books, movies, and music) are categorized specific to their associated SuperHero type. This means that if you chose the Freelancer path there are sets of books, movies, and music for you, just as there would be if you had chosen some other path. You probably have your own ideas about books, movies, and music that mean a lot to you and this is not meant to supplant or change that in any way. One way to look at these choices are like suggestions, little springboards to help you find the ones that work best for you. Like most of this book, you now have a starting point. Where you go from there is a choice I leave to you. If, on the other hand, you live under a rock and don't have choices of your own, perhaps just from a lack of exposure (as sub-rock housing tends to give a person), well, good luck with your new place in the sun; but I digress. As always feel free to pick and choose from any set or category you like. Either way they will definitely have something to offer.

One final note, the categories after each item listed are shown in descending order with the most relevant group listed first, and then they drop lower from there. So, for example if there were a listing of a movie that was shown classified as Free-Runner/Freelancer, it would have more relevance/uses/tips/concepts/ideas for the first category than it would for the second. In other words: they descend. As always, feel free to watch or read any of them regardless of your choice. The guidelines are just a suggestion.

MOVIES

➡ **THE MATRIX** *(Core/Flyer)*: For me, this is the movie that started it all. It's like a Consciousness Primer 101. This movie opened up the trains of thought of which I was just only barely aware. Interestingly enough, the 2nd and 3rd installments were dismal in comparison. The reason is simple: the filmmakers didn't know where to go. In the first one they had centuries of schools of thought to guide them, so the underlying message was there. However once the audience was brought to consciousness, the Wachowskis no longer had a guide. Neo finally realized that the world was what he said it was. Simple. But now where do you go?

The answer would have been to show the world that they are also the One. The world has always been what we say, and yet we get embroiled in this struggle. The better decision is to first realize your truth, and then realize that you are truth. What if everything around you was a metaphor and only you were the reality? What then? Either way, the filmmakers missed an opportunity.

➡ **WHAT THE BLEEP DO WE KNOW?!** *(Core/Flyer)*: This movie is basically The Matrix, part 2. I have even heard some people call it The Matrix User Manual. It adds a lot of validation and scientific fact to what would have otherwise been called just a good story (Matrix). It may seem redundant to continually say that this can really open up your mind but it really is all there for you to see, and well, yeah, it can really open up your mind. And yes, sometimes it is nice to see a little proof.

➡ **ELEKTRA** (Core/Flyer/Free-Runner): Realizing that a good review of a not-so-good movie brings with it a can of worms, I must ask for your thorough reading of this before you judge. For our purposes this is a good film for two reasons, one for the Core and one for the Flyer group. For the Flyers there's a character in the film named Tattoo. Tattoo is important because of the way his power manifests. Imagine sitting in meditation and having your thoughts interact with the world. Not only that, it is an illustration that our thoughts become things. Quantum Physics, Napoleon Hill, and Deepak Chopra all agree.

For the Core group we are looking at a completely different reason. The characters aren't explicitly born with traits, they can be taught them through the Martial Art known as Kimagure (imaginary, but you get the idea). Also, in the movie anyway, these powers are just accepted to be what they are, even for those who have never before experienced them. Good positive reinforcement for our new concepts.

As a final piece, the explanation that Stick gives of Kimagure is worth a listen for the Free-Runner not because Kimagure has classes every Tuesday and Thursday at the local YMCA, because it doesn't. What it shows you is that there is a lot about using energy in Martial Arts that has yet to be capitalized on. Fa Jing for example, or maybe Kyusho, to say nothing of Quantum Healing. All of these elements exist. Kimagure was just a fictional vehicle to showcase it. The real point being made here is that the disciplines themselves exist; just go find them.

➡ **EQUILIBRIUM** *(Free-Runner (or Freelancer, I suppose, but only if your job is Grammaton Cleric))*: Two words: Gun Kata. Ok, well yeah, there's more than two words... but seriously, if you know what Gun Kata is, then you know what I'm talking about. This movie was beautiful for the gun play (can you say that?). Also see UltraViolet for more instances of the action. Clearly this is for the Free-Runner group. As a word of warning, I don't suggest making your gun play elegant, in fact I don't suggest having gun play at all. What I do suggest is this however: if you are going to do something... do it magnificently.

➡ **PURSUIT OF HAPPYNESS** *(Freelancer)*: This, like many things in this book, makes sense once you see the connections. This movie, for our purposes, is aimed solely at the Freelancer group. Don't settle for your lot in life; make it, and everything around you, amazing. Go from Zero to Hero, don't take breaks needlessly, just focus... you'll be glad you did. And so will your child and your new fan base when people watch the movie of your life. Think it can't happen? This is the new reality, anything can happen. Let me ask you something, when Chris Gardner was sleeping in a bathroom in the subway, did he think he'd have a movie, or millions of dollars? Or did he think he could get beat up, arrested, shot, or worse? You tell me. He worked for it. So can you.

➡ **THE SECRET** *(Core/Freelancer/Free-Runner/Flyer)*: This movie has the widest usage so far. The Secret is all about attracting what you want in life. So if you want things in any of the categories, have them. The Secret shows you how. Apparently it was also a book. Don't know, never read it. What I do know is that it is right-on in a lot of respects. Life is yours for the making. It isn't challenging, it's a choice, nothing more. It's not even a decision. A decision implies laborious hours stuck in contemplation. A choice, eh, that's a quickie.

➡ **THE ASSIGNMENT** *(Free-Runner (or Freelancer depending on your job))*: This book could be a transcript of this movie. Verbatim. That is of course if they were about even remotely the same subject. One is a movie about Carlos the Jackal with the CIA in relentless pursuit and the other is (you guessed it) this book. What happens here that makes it powerful though is that the government takes an untrained individual and in a short amount of time trains them to become an amazing SuperHero that can take on the baddest of the bad. They also show some great training tips (with lots of extrapolation, mind you). The message, if Aidan Quinn can do it, why not you?

➡ **THE FOUNTAIN** *(Flyer)*: Has an overriding concept about the continuity of life that is very valuable. Also some excellent teaching from the bubble (watch it and see). The thousand year journey is of course only the beginning, but the rest of the trip is clearly outside the scope of this book. Look me up if you want to talk further.

➡ **THE BUTTERFLY EFFECT** *(Flyer)*: This movie surprised me for what it said about our control of events. Overall a strong message. The basic premise is that events are not set in stone even after we have experienced them. I support that. Change what you feel you must, just remember that everything is connected.

➡ **BATMAN BEGINS** *(Free-Runner/Core)*: Really strong for the Free-Runner group. Very physically based, similar to The Assignment in that someone who is basically untrained can change as they wish and then overcome, well, everything. There is a solid overriding message here as well: it's not who you are on the inside... it's what you do that matters. So get the hell off the couch. A message from this station and your local get the hell off the couch advisory board.

➡ **PHENOMENON** *(Core)*: The powers in this movie aren't themselves of interest as much as it is the way they are explained (in particular the agreement between substances) and the fact that an everyday Joe can, at least for a moment, absolutely shine.

➡ **SPY GAME** *(Free-Runner)*: Once again the theme of everyman being plucked from obscurity to learn some really cool stuff. Watching Redford play out his hand makes this movie an amazing experience for the aspiring Free-Runner (or Spy).

BOOKS

➡ **HOW TO BECOME A SUPERHERO**: Obviously.

➡ **THE NAVY SEAL WORKOUT BOOK** *(Core/Free-Runner)*: Take something sacred and make it accessible to the common man without it losing its sacred nature... sound like a contradiction? The Navy SEAL Workout Book does exactly this. The Navy SEALs have long been regarded as the pinnacle of military fitness, far beyond that of the mere mortal. This book makes it possible for anyone to reach this level of fitness with a quick routine that has been scientifically formulated to accomplish just that. Truly amazing.

➡ **JONATHON LIVINGSTON SEAGULL** *(Core)*: This is so not just a book about a bird. What are the boundaries of our reality? Why are those the boundaries, and not something else? What if we ran counter to our culture and changed, or even refused, our currently accepted belief system? That's what this book is about... and then asks the reader to figure out where from here. A truly inspiring read.

➡ **OBES IN 30 DAYS** *(Flyer/Free-Runner)*: Like The Navy SEAL Workout Book this manual takes the out of reach and delivers it up on a silver platter to those who would but apply themselves. Many excellent tricks and tips: like sitting in a movie theater before the movie and focusing on hearing only specific seats in different rows. Amazing use of the senses and a big step up for Spy Craft.

➡ **THE CELESTINE PROPHECY** *(Core)*: Belief system book, in a manner of speaking. There are a lot of beginner concepts in here that can serve to open up the world when you are ready. Things like the Aura, Past-Life Drama, Coincidences, etc... If you haven't yet read it then you should. Skip the workbook.

➡ **MOUNTAINS, MEADOWS AND MOONBEAMS: A CHILD'S SPIRITUAL READER** *(Flyer/Core)*: Little did I know about the huge amount of books for children that explain amazing concepts like magic and super powers. I will leave it up to you to find them... This book, in very simple terms, explains things like the Etheric, Astral Travel, Protective White Lights, you name it, this book has it. And it's cute too.

➡ **LUCID DREAMING** *(Flyer)*: I love that books like this even exist. Awaken completely in your dreams and explore your own subconscious using all the powers of reasoning and logic that you like. Go anywhere while in there, ask any question, it all becomes open to you. Learn to fly if you like, or try your hand at Dream-Spinning. You will find these skills valuable. What would you ask the most powerful computer on the planet if you had the opportunity? Well now here's your chance.

➡ **LUCID LIVING: A Book You Can Read in an Hour That Will Turn Your World Inside Out** *(Core/Flyer)*: Wake up, it's all been a dream. Your job, your life, your friends... none of it real. It tries to answer in a nutshell what has taken some people their entire lives. Seriously, why wait? Use the microwave. Just kidding, I love the book, and I firmly agree with the concept.

➡ **EMMANUEL'S BOOK: A Manual for Living Comfortably in the Cosmos** *(Flyer)*: This book will absolutely free your mind... but only when you are ready for it. Strictly a Flyer's only book for that reason. A strong read with amazing answers to a great many things... if you can handle it.

➡ **ROLLING THUNDER: Turning Junk Into Automobile Weaponry** *(Free-Runner)*: Actually an interesting read, even if you're not a Free-Runner. I learned more about—Here, just let the author tell you: (Paraphrased from the book)

> *blinding lights, smoke screens, tire busters, mines deployed from moving car, oil slicks, firearms fired remotely... seat belts that electrically shock a hostile passenger... Requires only common tools and the simplest of materials found in any workshop scrap pile,*

—than I ever hoped to or needed to.

➡ **SPEED READING MADE EASY** *(Core/Freelancer)*: This is a must have skill. Once you possess this skill you have access to anything found in books at speeds many times faster than almost anyone else. School books, homework, business proposals, office projects: Owned.

➡ **DRIVE TO SURVIVE** *(Free-Runner)*: Paraphrased from the book: evasive driving techniques, bootlegger hairpin, J-turns, running assailants off the road… with combat survival and race car driving techniques. What more can you ask for when you are behind the wheel of a car? Use this power only for good.

MUSIC

➡ **MAN OF LA MANCHA (Song 2) I, Don Quixote; Richard Kiley**: See Below.

➡ **THE IMPOSSIBLE DREAM (Song 11) The Quest; Richard Kiley**: Both of these are truly inspirational. Such power in Kiley's voice and an excellent message as well.

➡ **BREAKAWAY; Kelly Clarkson**: Spirited song… take a chance.

➡ **KILL BILL VOLUME ONE - Battle Without Honor or Humanity; Tomoyasu Hotei**: Instrumental. The point with music, and in fact any of the suggestions here, find what inspires you—what truly inspires you—and use that. You'll be glad you did.

Appendix 2

A Word About SuperHeroes

❝ A SuperHero.

Simply defined:
One who makes heroic history,
One who is portrayed as an ideal or role-model.

But is this only in a book with funny writing?
Or alive in real life?

This answer is up to the beholder.

Some say one must have powers
That no others hold.

Some say one must have the power of adrenaline
That never stops.

I SAY:
The person who teaches you to walk is a hero
As they are preparing you for walking down the aisle.

SAY:
The person who teaches you to read is a hero
As they are preparing you for all kinds of knowledge to be learned as the future comes.

SAY:
The person who teaches you to talk is a hero
As they are preparing you for speaking all kinds of languages and traveling the world.

But most importantly,
YOU are the hero.

For you have the ability to
SEE beyond,
HEAR beyond,
and LEARN beyond your tiny little crib and blanket.

Someone who is able to bring you into a world full of fascinating color, sound, taste, and smells
is someone who counts more than a character who can WALK THROUGH FIRE.

It takes more than two lines on the side of your cheeks to make a person happy.

And one who can accomplish that,
Is indeed
A Hero.

- Celeste -
12 years old, 7th grade

❝ When this concept of this book was first brought to me, I could barely contain my excitement about its truth, timeliness and importance.

Throughout my day, I feel a nagging force that ever so gently tugs at my insides. Some days I feel its pull stronger than others, though I often silence it with the continual distractions of our globalized pop culture world. I believe very strongly that I am fated to make great social change. I am driven by my love for humanity and idealistic belief that people can and do change the world. I dream of the day when others will include my name in conversations of Nelson Mandela, Che Guevara and Arundhati Roy. Yet, I have repeatedly ignored the calls for help and the chances to step up and act. I have talked myself out of opportunities that did not seem plausible and taken short cuts when I thought it didn't matter. This passivity kills me, as I'm sure it has to so many others. I understand not everyone feels this way, and so this concept and this book are not for them. It's okay, let them sleep.

We are terrified of our own immortality, constantly beating ourselves down into a corner and rejecting our abilities. Even with all the advancements we've made with technology, music, literature, and science, we still all just want to "get by." Personally, I think there's way more fun to be had. It was these realizations that "opened" me. We have to stop convincing ourselves that our talents are limited and our bodies are insignificant. Changing the world does not have to be a vague, distant fantasy that I never take seriously. Instead, I have made it a real aim that I consider in everything that I do. I am currently going through my own process of becoming a superhero, setting specific goals and teaching myself new things. The process is by no means easy; my steps are slow and uncertain. But I have been opened and will not shut myself out.

Don't let yourself be led by your fears or cowardice. Be led by your passion. Be led by what makes your blood rush and your eyes fill with tears.

Elizabeth,

UC Santa Cruz

66 I would want to be invisible and have telekinesis and my name would be Intel.

Jonathan, *Age 13*

66 If I were a superhero my name would be Speedy. My powers would be super speed, telekinesis and x ray vision. I would be a hero and fight crime. I would stop robbers, stop littering and theft of cars.

Garrett, *Age 10*

 Can you change the world?

Da Vinci was the bastard son of a peasant woman.

Einstein was just a clerk in the patent office.

Shakespeare was just a writer.

J.K. Rowling was a welfare mother.

Van Gogh suffered from depression and sometimes acted out violently.

Red Cloud and Geronimo had no formal education.

Elvis was a truck driver who lived in poverty while his dad was in prison.

Ludwig Van Beethoven was deaf.

Martin Luther King, Jr. was just a preacher... not a rich businessman... not president.

Mother Theresa never held an office.

Gandhi never made a million dollars.

Jesus of Nazareth did not start with a million followers... He had 12, 11 if you don't count Judas. He was just a carpenter.

Tell them you can't change the world. Do you think they had all the advantages? Success is not measured by where you come from or what you have been born into. We all can do the best we can with what little we've got at the time.

Angel,

Miami, FL